FRANCISCO ROMERO
ON PROBLEMS OF PHILOSOPHY

Francisco Romero on Problems of Philosophy

by

MARJORIE S. HARRIS

RANDOLPH-MACON WOMAN'S COLLEGE

PHILOSOPHICAL LIBRARY

New York

© Copyright, 1960,
by Philosophical Library, Inc.
15 East 40th Street, New York

199.82
R763Y
H315f

Printed in the United States of America

To Rodney

PREFACE

Like Hamlet, Francisco Romero has found his time "out of joint," but he has not bemoaned the necessity which he regards as laid upon him to provide what assistance a profound thinker can give toward setting things right; he has accepted that task philosophically. Is the crisis of our time due to the failure of man to understand himself? There are those who believe that such is the case. If this be so, any light that can be thrown on the essential nature of man is a prime requisite for today. This is one of the problems to which Romero contributes his own, deep insight in order to bring closer to realization a genuine solution. And there are other problems which have become less enigmatic because of his strenuous exploration of their perplexing natures. In presenting Romero's views on these matters, I have held rather closely to the texts, where I have not actually quoted, in order to present as adequate an introduction as possible to aspects of Romero's philosophy.

Now it is my pleasure to express my indebtedness to various persons. First and foremost I am very deeply grateful to Professor Francisco Romero for his permission to translate statements from his various works for use in this book. And most of all I am very much indebted to him for his gracious encouragement as the work has progressed and for the books, journals, and bulletins which he has sent me. He has read an article of mine, published in PHILOSOPHY AND PHENOMENOLOGICAL RESEARCH, March, 1955. From this article I have taken sections and incorporated them in Chapter V, with the kind permission of Professor Marvin

Farber, editor of that journal. Professor Romero has also read chapters I, VI and the major part of VII—except for the first paragraph or two and the last one or two paragraphs in each chapter, introduced to tie the chapters together, as it were. Of this article and of these chapters Professor Romero has written as follows and has given me permission to present in this preface a translation of his generous commendation: "You have seen with penetration and exactitude the points of my writings which you have taken into account, and I can not but felicitate myself that I have received concerning them an exegesis so able and adequate."

I am also indebted to three editors for their kind permission to use excerpts from articles of mine published in their journals. Professor Emerson Buchanan has given me permission to make use of sections of an article published in the JOURNAL OF PHILOSOPHY on April 9, 1953. These sections are in chapter II. Professor Louis Kattsoff has granted me the privilege of using parts of an article which appeared in his THE SOUTHERN PHILOSOPHER, September, 1952. These sections are incorporated in chapter IV. As I have already stated in the foregoing paragraph, Professor Marvin Farber has written that I might use whatever I chose to use from an article which was published in PHILOSOPHY AND PHENOMENOLOGICAL RESEARCH, March, 1955. The sections which I have chosen appear in chapter V.

I am fortunate to have the privilege of using quotations from Dr. Dagobert Runes's ON THE NATURE OF MAN. My thanks are due Professor James K. Feibleman for allowing me to quote from his article, "Toward an Analysis of the Basic Value Systems." To Professor Cornelius Krusé I wish to express my appreciation—as well as to Professor Romero—for permission to quote from Professor Romero's paper, presented at the Second Inter-American Congress of Philosophy and published in the Proceedings. At that time Professor Krusé was President of the Congress and Chairman of the Board of Officers.

From the Yale University Press I have their kind permission to quote from E. Cassirer's AN ESSAY ON MAN, and also to quote from F. S. C. Northrop's IDEOLOGICAL

DIFFERENCES AND WORLD ORDER. The article from which I have quoted in the book edited by Professor Northrop is one by Professor Romero and I also have his gracious permission to quote from any of his writings.

Various publishing companies have kindly allowed me to quote sentences from books which they have published. Dr. Harry Snowden, Jr. of P. F. Collier & Son Corporation very kindly wrote that I did not need permission to quote from Thomas Huxley's "Science and Culture," which was published in the HARVARD CLASSICS.

The Macmillan Company is generously allowing me to quote from Matthew Arnold's CULTURE AND ANARCHY, New York, 1925 and copyrighted in 1925.

My thanks are due to W. W. Norton & Co., Inc. for giving me the right to quote from M. Adam's translation of Ortega y Gasset's INVERTEBRATE SPAIN, New York, 1937.

The Philosophical Library is granting me the privilege of quoting from Dagobert Runes's ON THE NATURE OF MAN, New York, 1956, and for this permission I am very grateful to them and to Dr. Runes.

G. P. Putnam's Sons & Coward-McCann, Inc. have given permission to quote from John Dewey's ART AS EXPERIENCE, Minton, Balch & Co., 1934—copyrighted by John Dewey in 1934: I thank them.

Charles Scribner's Sons have expressed willingness for me to quote from their Descartes, SELECTIONS, New York, 1927 and for this I thank them.

David McKay Company, Inc. has kindly permitted me to quote from Thomas Mann's THE LIVING THOUGHTS OF SCHOPENHAUER.

Professor Maria de Onate, a relative of Ortega y Gasset, helped me most graciously until her retirement from the faculty of Randolph-Macon Woman's College when I had a problem in translation.

Miss Evelyn Harvey and Miss Dorothy Ford gave secretarial assistance when I was pressed for time and for this help I am most grateful.

And finally I am in the enduring debt of those students

who have studied Latin American philosophy with me. My appreciation goes especially to the following former majors in the department who have rendered valuable secretarial or other help: Mrs. Robert L. Alwood, Mrs. James A. H. Ferguson, Mrs. Clyde H. Wilkinson, and Miss Carol Kingman. Mrs. John F. Foster, Jr. was also a valuable assistant. I wish to make especial mention of the help given by Mrs. Alwood. She lived in Peru during her childhood and early youth so that I have found her help in translation invaluable. These last two and one half years she has given unstintingly of her time whenever I appealed to her for assistance and it has meant very much to me to be able always to count on that aid and that interest in the progress of the book.

Marjorie Silliman Harris

Lynchburg, Virginia

CONTENTS

Preface	vii
Introduction	1
On the Problematic Approach to Philosophy	28
Cartesian Reason	39
On Minimal Man	49
On the Dual Nature of Man	63
Transcendence	74
Toward an Ontology of Culture	84
On the Current, General Crisis	97
Epilogue	115

INTRODUCTION

In order to be adequately prepared to comprehend the important contributions of Francisco Romero to the central concerns of philosophy, one should know something of his life. This claim is in line with the Fichtean dictum which states that the kind of philosophy which a man espouses depends upon the kind of man he is. This dictum is recalled by Romero during his philosophizing on the history of philosophy. First, then, we shall proceed to note pertinent details in the life of Romero.

He was born in Seville in 1891 but came, at an early age, with his parents to Argentina. His first career was a military one but, even while an army officer, he studied philosophy and in 1928 was appointed *Profesor Suplente* at the University of Buenos Aires. A year later he was given a simlar post at the University of La Plata. In 1931 Romero retired from the army after having attained a high rank.

The years following this retirement have been filled with many important activities as teacher, as writer, as administrator, as editor, and as a devoted citizen striving to promote the welfare of his country. Thus Romero has exemplified in his way of life the application of the view held by him and by other Latin American thinkers that the university man should not be too exclusively devoted to a speciality; that he must do his part toward solving political and social problems.[1] Upon Romero's retirement from the army he was made *Profesor Titular* at the University of Buenos Aires and in 1936 he was given the same rank at the University of La

Plata. Subsequently he added to his professorial duties by becoming professor of the theory of scientific knowledge at the *Instituto Nacional del Profesorado*. He has taken an active interest in the *Colegio Libro de Estudios Superiores* since its founding in 1931 and was appointed to the Alejandro Korn chair in that institution in 1940. He has declined offers of academic posts in the United States, Mexico, Cuba, and Chile. In 1946 Romero resigned from teaching because of fundamental differences with the government of Perón. It is good to know that Romero is now back taking an active part in reorganizing university life, in guiding the affairs of the *Sociedad Filosófica Argentina* as its president, participating in the reorganization of the *Facultad de Filosofía y Letras de Buenos Aires*, Director of the *Departamento de Filosofía de la Facultad*, Director of the *Instituto de Filosofía* of the same, member of the Council of the Faculty, and in general taking a leading part in erasing the ravages of a tyrannical regime.

In spite of his administrative work and his heavy teaching schedule, Romero has found time through the years to write extensively. His first articles appeared in 1916 and many other articles and books have followed those first published writings. He has also edited the writings of others. Thus in 1938 he was invited to become the director of *Biblioteca Filosófica* of *Editorial Losada*. He is the founder of the review, Realidad, and at its inception became its editor.

As a citizen, Romero has sought to promote the wellbeing of his fellow countrymen. One example of such efforts is his work as a member of the organizing commission of *ASCUA*, i.e., the *Asociación Cultural Argentina para Defensa y Superación de Mayo*. This association was organized in 1952 by a group of patriots who sought to clarify and affirm "the most profound tradition of Argentina: this is the tradition of liberty within the democracy as a basis for progress."[2]

Romero's outstanding achievements have won for him eminently deserved laurels, among these the following: the Vaccaro prize, the *Gran Premio de Honor de la Sociedad Argentina de Escritores*, and, on the first occasion when awards were given for scientific and literary work after the liberation from the tyranny of Perón, the first prize in one of the four groups honored was given to Romero for his *Teoría del Hombre*.[3]

So much for a brief survey of some of the many activities of Francisco Romero and for a mention of a few of the honors showered upon him for his signal achievements. Even so short a survey as this one gives evidence of the fact that he did not fall into what he regards as Descartes' error of isolating himself from the world of affairs after his sojourn in the army. Clearly Romero richly merits the recognition he has received in being acclaimed the Dean of Latin American Philosophers.[4]

From this brief resumé of details in the life of a great American we turn to a statement of the purpose of this study. That purpose is to present Romero's views on certain fundamental problems of philosophy. The reason for centering attention on problems is that Romero believes in the problematic rather than in the constructive or systematic approach to philosophy. He thinks that the age of system making is past; that the philosopher's business is that of dealing with problems unfettered by a preconceived scheme into which findings must fit.[5] Indeed philosophy should proceed without entangling presuppositions, otherwise it would be—Romero thinks—very like a man trying to rid himself of his shadow. This exposition is undertaken in spite of the fact that only a reading of Romero's own writings will enable one fully to appreciate the penetrating thought of this great philosopher. However, our hope is that this exposition will present so faithfully aspects of Romero's thought that the reader will not be satisfied until he has become better acquainted with the wisdom of this American sage through the reading of his own works.

As for procedure in this introduction, it has seemed best to marshal here certain views of Romero which will not be developed in the chapters to follow. Before doing that, however, attention should be called to one statement quoted with approval by Romero, for the thought so succinctly throws light on his own breadth of vision: " 'He who knows only philosophy does not even know philosophy.' " Comment would be superfluous.

Now a brief note on philosophy of yesteryear in Spanish America and specifically in Argentina is in order as a background against which to see Romero's own views. In Ibero-America, Romero points out, general interest in philosophy did not develop until the recent past. The reason for this lack of general interest is as follows. After the countries gained their independence, it was natural that thinkers should be concerned with practical matters; or with historical events which would clarify the situation which had preceded the liberation; or with literary creations which portrayed the men and the life in these countries. As a consequence of this earlier preoccupation, "the founders of Latin American philosophy . . . , save for isolated cases, were those belonging to the positivistic stage and to the subsequent anti-positivistic movement."[6] A considerable portion of the philosophical work in these countries has been a criticism of positivism. Foremost among the Argentine thinkers refuting positivism have been Alejandro Korn and Coriolanus Alberini. Korn had a certain respect for the adversary which he was so effective in dethroning even though he felt that Argentina needed a philosophy which stressed enduring values rather than material ones. Furthermore, Korn saw that positivism was not simply the brain child of Comte and Spencer. Romero quotes with approval Korn's statement that positivism is not " 'an artificial creation of its exponents but first of all, in the past century, it was the spiritual attitude common to all the Occident, born and diffused under the sway of the same historical situation.' "[7] Romero adds that the indigenous positivism of Argentina was especially influential in primary education and prepared the way for the imported type of positivism. The Comtean positivism brought a new interpretation of psychology with emphasis on experimental work. Also this positivism promoted interest in sociology and even stimulated concern for the development of the other sciences. Hence positivism was to an extent beneficial. Thus Korn's attitude of appreciation for what positivism did accomplish was an attitude which was not blinded by this recognition of the defects of positivism.

On the other hand, Alberini's critique of positivism was

too acrimonious, Romero thinks, especially as Alberini tended to overlook the benefits contributed by positivism.* Moreover, the very shortcomings of positivism had a salutary effect since the polemics against them prepared the way for developments of "points of view more in tune with the new era."[8] Even so, the attacks on positivism did hinder developments in psychology and sociology. Furthermore, a special value of the positivistic era should be mentioned: positivism did supply a unitary view of the world. Such a unitary outlook had not been achieved since the Middle Ages—an outlook made up of a series of connected and harmonious beliefs. Lacking an achievement of this kind "the men of the West were without firm convictions on which to rest; without common principles to bind them together; without security before the enigma of the cosmos."[9] Hence positivism made a genuine contribution in this respect. So much for the debits and credits of positivism, as Romero evaluates them.

Not only did the coming of Comtean positivism to Argentina result in new philosophical developments but also the coming of Ortega y Gasset in 1916 contributed to the creation of a new climate of views in philosophy. Ortega

---

* Alberini, in his *Die Deutsche Philosophie in Argentinien*, pp. 51-58, offers very sharp criticisms of positivism. These criticisms may be summed up as follows. He thinks that Comte's positivism was backward for Europe even at the time it was promulgated and that this philosophy was especially damaging to his native country because that country lacked the tradition for close and exact thought. He thinks that the positivism fostered in Argentina was positivism at its worst. In Argentina Comtean positivists placed little value on the fundamental problems of philosophy; whereas what his native country needed was a philosophy which encouraged philosophical and scientific research—not a philosophy which paralyzed the wings of pure research and asked only useful questions. Alberini thinks that one reason why such a philosophy was developed was that there was economic progress. At least the brilliant period of positivism was coincident with that progress. Positivism provided an elegant, shallow instruction for the leaders of the rich, new society that had found wealth so easy to procure and felt so secure about the future. Education in positivism encouraged dilettantism; stimulated interest in rhetorical form, regardless of the ideas expressed; was responsible for the growth of amoral literature. Furthermore, positivism hindered—as already implied—the development of pure science because it did not encourage exact thinking, which is so essential for carrying on genuine, scientific investgation. Such, in substance, is Dr. Alberini's critique of positivism.

stimulated interest in his own philosophy as well as interest in German philosophy and especially in the philosophy of Kant.[10] When it was reported in 1936 that Ortega would again visit Buenos Aires, Romero wrote enthusiastically of the enrichment which that visit would bring to those who would have the privilege of hearing him and conversing with him. Romero pointed out that "the Spanish Philosopher has the will to inform himself about all intellectual or vitally important events which occur in the whole world."[11] Romero extolled Ortega's intellectual curiosity and his urge to investigate other points of view, for which reasons his work exhibits "richness and variety." In the past his teaching had been both "stimulating and instructive" to his hearers, who had been attracted by his disciplined and energetic thought.[12]

Although Ortega did influence Argentine thought, Romero states that the person who had the greatest influence on the development of his own thought was Alejandro Korn— a physician, the director of a hospital for the mentally ill, and a philosopher. For Romero, the brief eulogy of Socrates offered by Phaedo in reporting the death of his master can be aptly applied to Korn*—"of all those . . . whom it has been given us to know he was the best and the wisest and the justest." Like Socrates, Korn had a great capacity for friendship. His friendliness was of a very elevated sort for he respected the desire of his close friends for a certain amount of privacy and hence did not pry into their innermost lives. In this respect his thought was at one with that of Ralph Waldo Emerson. Furthermore, he helped another to hope when such optimism was reasonable, but dissipated the irrational hope of a person when the event required that Korn give a precise judgment which was contrary to the fond wishes of that other. Korn was able to do this effectively because he saw beyond the flux of things as they appear to the permanent and the stable. That insight—achieved early in life—was the reason for his triumphant optimism, even though he had witnessed "the harsh drama of life" as director of a hospital for the insane. And that sane optimism he was

---

* Alejandro Korn, *Filósofo de la Libertad*, p. 7.

able to radiate to others. Indeed he helped others quite as much by example as by admonition; that is, he had an "affable and majestic countenance," a keen sense of humor, a robust character, and a good will—which was the "ordering principle of his life."[13]

In Korn that good will was joined to an intellect of great power and this was one of the reasons why he became a great philosopher. As is characteristic of a philosopher as well as a scientist, he had a passion for facts and from facts his thought penetrated to the universal which is back of the facts. Indeed, in his early life he had been able, Romero says, to achieve an insight into the heart of things and, as a consequence, "no disaster could overwhelm him." This penetrating insight is reflected in one of his statements on Kant, a statement which Romero quotes as a kind of "intimate confession" on the part of Korn. This statement is as follows: " 'Beyond the immensity of the starry sky or in the intimate feeling which moves the human heart, the trembling thinker has a presentiment of the inaccessible key of the grand enigma.' "[14] But the robust intelligence of Korn—though recognizing the limits of the human mind, as evidenced by the expression, "trembling thinker,"—was not perturbed by such limitation for Korn fully appreciated the dignity of the human person because Korn saw beyond the superficial exterior and achieved an appreciation of man as he was born to be. Korn saw the human person as "the culmination of reality" at a time when the tendency on the part of many was to value the things produced rather than he who was responsible for such production. These persons who placed supreme value on things failed to realize that the creation of a life worth living was more important than the making of things. For Korn the central problem of philosophy is the person and the essence of the person is liberty. Hence Romero has referred to Korn as the Philosopher of Liberty. Romero points out that, for Korn, "the essential in man is his constitutional rebellion against any compulsion, as much against that which comes from outside as against that born within him." Korn saw as hindrances to freedom the desire for gain and for power; the urge to grasp even violently whatever might make for self-aggrandizement; in short, egoistical drives. These, quite as much as outside curbs, could enslave man. Hence through his teaching and through his writing and, above all, through his way of life, he tried to make clear what liberty means. In Korn's mind, his lectures and his conversations were a more important way of conveying his message than his writings, for, like Socrates, Korn believed that the spoken word is more important than the written word. Yet Korn did leave "written work of notable value." His original contributions were in the fields of epistemology and axiology.[15] But his greatest contribution was the kind of life which he lived, expressing in that life those highest values about which he spoke and wrote. With Korn in mind, Romero said—on the third anniversary of the death of this majestic personality: "Exceptional men perform the function of making patent to others those transcendental realities, invisible to physical eyes. . . . But the manly exemplar reveals the hidden and converts himself into model and guide; not as the commanding officer who orders but as the light which reveals the way in darkness."

With these few notations concerning what Romero says of Korn as man and as philosopher, it is obviously impossible to convey adequately to the reader the nobility and grandeur of one of the great Americans of all time. But the hope is that these brief paragraphs will arouse an interest in the inspiring life and penetrating thought of Alejandro Korn and that they will encourage others to read all the word-portraits painted by his most illustrious pupil, Francisco Romero.

For that pupil, what is philosophy? We should first of all keep in mind Romero's interest in furthering widespread interest in philosophy. Such stimulation of interest is very important for, while it is true that "he who knows only philosophy does not even know philosophy," it is also true that he who does not know philosophy does philosophize and does at times indulge in pseudo-philosophic excogitation, which makes only a faulty road-bed on which to run a train of thought. Hence it is very necessary that the nature of philosophizing be understood. How, then, does Romero answer the question: what is philosophy? He points out that there is no definition which will be universally satisfactory but says that it is usual to think of the customary branches of philosophy as attempts to attain ultimate and total knowledge. For such achievement one must turn his back on the everyday habit of accepting things at their face value and of judging these things only in terms of their practical value. One must "estrange himself from the world," must survey it as a strange, new world—seeking by this means to pierce through to the hidden reality. Romero also notes that it has been said that philosophy begins with no presuppositions, whereas science does begin with presuppositions—such as: the existence of the world, of space and time, of the efficacy of certain methods. Romero holds that the view that philosophy is "before all knowledge without presuppositions" is not a statement which applies to philosophies as they are. He cites fundamental assumptions of historical systems to support his assertion—such as the dogmatic rationalism of some ancient and modern systems of philosophy. And he suggests that it may be "the mark of philosophy as an ideal" to reflect critically without presuppositions.[16]

In view of this suggested contrast between philosophy and science, one is prepared for Romero's assertion that philosophy is not simply a "complement of science." The logical positivist has shrunken philosophy as he understands it to that dimension. But philosophy will not be so shrunken and, on the other hand, it needs no sanforizing process to enable it to fulfill its own, proper rôle. For Romero, philosophy is not the hand-maid of science. But science does raise philosophical questions many times and he thinks that there is "a logical sequence between the knowledge of the sciences and that of philosophy." Thus, for example, "in its most profound capacity, that of interpretation . . . , physics abandons the plane of the sensible (the visible, audible, tangible, *etc.*) and seeks an intelligent or rational explanation of facts." This procedure calls for a theory of knowledge. Furthermore, this necessity for a theory of knowledge is an evidence of the continuity of knowledge—knowledge "which points to a harmonious and plausible vision of totality, knowledge with which man appears not to be able to dispense."[17]

As for attempting to say what constitutes the various, usual branches of philosophy, Romero thinks that such an attempt is idle because a statement about the present situation in these areas might not even now be the way in which some thinkers view these branches and certainly it would be highly questionable whether one could say much which would be true in those areas in the future, because great thinkers have chosen to emphasize those problems which seem to them of prime importance and have neglected other problems.[18] One branch of philosophy in which Romero is especially interested is anthropological philosophy. He notes that the problems in this area were sharpened in the middle of the nineteenth century. Then the foundation of the anthropological doctrine was believed to be natural science. Now, however, the realization has developed that "the anthropological philosophy of our day does not give the lie to the results of biology but maintains that mere biology is incapable of giving a complete account of the human being."[19] We shall have much more to say about this aspect of Romero's thought in a later chapter.

From these points made by Romero in presenting an introductory discussion of what philosophy is, we shall turn to indicate very sketchily his views on certain problems of philosophy. First, however, we must say something about personalism for, as we noted in an earlier footnote, Romero has been called a personalist.* Also we have noted his opposition to systems. Hence we have concluded that, on that score alone if for no other reason, he would not care to be categorized as a personalist. However there are other reasons, which we shall indicate briefly. In a certain sense, Romero thinks that personalism is "a direction of thought which sees in personality the supreme key to philosophical problems both metaphysical and axiological." Yet, "in a more restricted sense, personalism is that philosophical position which defines being in terms of personal consciousness." Still, this would be too restricted a meaning for all personalists since Bright-

---

* *Cf.* footnote 5 and also Jose Franquiz's interesting discussion of what he regards as aspects of personalism in Romero's thought. *Cf.* REVISTA CUBANA DE FILOSOFIA, Vol. II, No. 9, pp. 21 ff.

man, for example, admitted a kind of realism such as that found in Aristotle. This is a realism "which does not reduce all existence to the personal consciousness but assigns to personality the sovereign place and the most elevated significance in all reality."[20] Romero points out that there have been many great thinkers sympathetic with this view that the person is of supreme importance. We should add that Romero himself subscribes to this appraisal of the person.

After making these general statements about personalism Romero proceeds to mention some of the most important features of personalism, in the strict sense, as set forth in Brightman's description of this school of thought. We shall mention here two of these features together with Romero's position on them. However, Romero's resumé of these two features is not followed by his own reaction to them. It is we who are juxtaposing his opinions stated elsewhere. In this connection it is very important as an aid to the recognition of Romero as a great and magnanimous thinker to note that he apparently shares Comte's theory that "all men are collaborators in the search for truth." With Romero that view is not only in his head but in his heart—as Hegel would have said. Now what are these two features of personalism to which reference has been made and what is Romero's position on each of them? Romero states that for the typical personalist "all that exists is spirit or exists for, in, or by spirit."[21] But for Romero *individual*—with his self-centered aims—exists as much as the spiritual person. It is true that *individual* should put his energies at the service of the spiritual in him, should "bear the yoke" of spirit and thus should exist for spirit, but this is not always the case—as we shall note in a later chapter. Romero points out that the Greek word for *person* "alludes to the mask which covers the face of the actor." Analogously, *person*—that is, the spiritual in man—is superposed on *individual* and constitutes, as it were, a new being who does not obey "the conveniences, the tastes, and the interests of *individual*" but this new being voluntarily submits itself to an order of values which transcends it and "from the steadfastness and stability of these values is derived the firmness and stability of *person*." Thus *person* covers the "changing flow of impulses and appetites of *individual*" as the "immutable mask covers the changing expressions of the countenance of the actor."[22] Yet, "when *person* subordinates *individual* to himself, he is not placing a fiction over a reality but placing a most high reality over another of less dignity."[23] Thus the implication is that *individual* does exist and does not always exist "for, in, or by the spirit"—or the spiritual person, the typical personalist to the contrary.

The other feature of personalism which should be discussed here is Brightman's thesis that spiritual experience is rational experience even though he does not mean *rational* experience in the sense in which it is frequently meant—i.e., as "predominately logical and mathematical experience" but by rational experience Brightman means "a harmonious, all-comprehensive, consistent, and orderly experience."[24] From Romero's point of view, at the center of spiritual activity is the will. Thus our "spiritual faculties—cognitive, aesthetic, *etc.*—are composed as a circle in whose center is the will as spiritual activity. . . . The volitional moment functions within each spiritual activity and determines it." "The spiritual attitude, then, resolves itself into a bundle of spiritual acts." Moreover, "the will to realize these acts is the nucleus of the person."[25] But this will is not the will as conceived by a Schopenhauer or by a Thomas Mann when he comments on Schopenhauer. This will is not "a fundamental unholiness, . . . an unrest, a striving for something." This will posited by Romero is not "want, craving, avidity, demand, suffering." It is not such a will that of it Mann can say that "a world of will can be nothing else but a world of suffering."[26] This will to which Romero refers is a will that is determined to bring into being values. This will is the kind of will that found expression in the way of life of Romero's great teacher, Alejandro Korn, with his "active, energetic, militant goodness." And it is this type of will which enables Romero to perform his magnificent services to his country—we certainly should add.

Besides these specific points on which Romero and the North American personalists do not see eye to eye, there is a further difference between them. The personalists tend to ignore Royce, Romero thinks, and regard Bowne as their founder, whereas Romero classifies Royce as "in his way" a personalist.[27] Romero ranks Royce's *The World and the Individual* as perhaps "the greatest contribution of America to universal philosophy." Romero thinks that, in this great work, Royce has succeeded in showing that, whereas "finite being is an expression of the Divine Will, it is at the same time the expression here and now of its own will."[28] Romero praises Royce's accomplishment in *The Spirit of Modern Philosophy* because Royce has been "an impartial and severe judge" of the great figures in philosophy, whereas the tendency on the part of German thinkers has been to revere these men and hence to portray "the majestic heroes of thought" with the "rigid and artificial appearance of statues." Royce, on the other hand, has pictured these thinkers "in their everyday clothes" and thus has humanized them and at the same time has humanized philosophy in a way "which redounds to its dignity and its justification; to the triumphal defense of its value and its meaning regardless of the diversity of opinions and the contrast of systems." Romero quotes with approval Royce's statement, made in the first lecture in this book, that " 'the assumption upon which these lectures are based is . . . that philosophy is not a presumptuous effort to explain the mysteries of the world by means of any superhuman insight or extraordinary cunning, but it has its origin and value in an attempt to give a reasonable account of our own personal attitude towards the more serious business of life.' " Furthermore, Royce in 1900 viewed "our actual philosophy not so much as a giving up of the true spirit of any period but as a maturing and fixing of its more profound interests." This view is one that Romero voiced thirty years later without knowing at the time of Royce's pronouncement.[29]

This brief discussion of personalism has been presented to emphasize points in Romero's own thought; his appreciation of the supreme value of spiritual person while mindful, at the same time, of the inevitable striving of *person* to transcend the natural impulses and transitory desires of *individual;* his view of the spiritual experience as not merely a rational experience but also as one in which the will is at the center of the spiritual experience. However Romero is at one with the personalistic view that person is the most important aspect of reality. Moreover, we noted that Romero points out some of the significant insights of Royce, whom Romero regards as the most important of the personalists. Among these insights, we called attention to the following: the autonomy of the person who yet is an expression of the Divine Will; the candid evaluation of the real contribution of the great philosophers, together with Royce's modest appraisal of what he himself had to offer; his understanding of the relation of current philosophy to the thought of the past, noting that, at the present time, there is not so much a turning of the back on what the past has to contribute as a more mature appreciation of what really counts. Hence he finds a genuine continuity between current philosophy and the philosophies of yesteryear.

Romero himself has much of interest to say concerning the history of philosophy and we turn now to indicate a few of the points which he has made. He maintains that "the historical and the current interest in philosophy are inseparable" because culture is not static but is in flux. As a consequence, "in each of its moments and products, even in the ones appearing most rigid and stable, there are latent, hidden tensions, deposits, and ferments of the past."[30] Romero goes on to observe that there is much more interest among philosophers in the history of philosophy than is true of the interest of men in other disciplines in the histories of their given fields. Furthermore, this interest of philosophers has increased prodigiously in recent times. And he finds it true that some philosophers are interested in the history of philosophy for its own sake, while other philosophers regard the history of philosophy as an effective aid for "the understanding and resolving" of questions which have arisen. Romero thinks that frequently the whole development of philosophy throws light on current problems.[31]

It is natural, then, that he should regard as "one of the most fertile directions of present thought the philosophical examination of the history of philosophy."[32] He goes on to point out two important results which such a critical examination has had. In the first place, some names and works which were regarded as significant in the past do not even appear in current histories of philosophy, whereas the works of some other men are now held in higher esteem than was the case formerly. For example, De Gérando wrote his *Histoire de la Philosophie Moderne* in the first third of the nineteenth century. Some thinkers who were given considerable space in that work are not even mentioned today whereas men like Spinoza had only a few notes on their work in De Gérando's book. The reason for this change is partly due to the fact that material, once lost sight of, has become available with the passage of time. Two illustrations will suffice here. During the Renaissance, Greek texts—unknown during the Middle Ages—were brought to Western Europe.* Again, Pedro Hispano—who became Pope John XXI—wrote a book, *De Anima*, which was discovered in a Spanish library in 1927. This book throws light on the psychological theories of the Middle Ages. Another reason for this change in the evaluation of the contributions of earlier philosophers is the change in the climate of opinion. Hence what appeared significant once does not seem so now and what was regarded as of little value once is now held in higher favor. Since this is the case, Romero believes that, in the future, the histories of philosophy will be different because the philosophical works of the past will be seen from a new perspective.

A second result of the critical examination of the history of philosophy is that, in certain cases, there is now more doubt about the accuracy of our knowledge of the thought of certain great men than was the case formerly. This is

---

* It will be recalled that Gemisthus Plethon came to Italy in 1438 to attend a church council called by Pope Eugenius IV. While in Florence, Gemisthus aroused the interest of Cosimo de Medici in Plato. As one consequence, Cosimo had a whole staff of men seeking important manuscripts in the East and thus acquired a great library. Cosimo heard a medical student read a paper on Plato. This student was Marsilio Ficino, a son of Cosimo's physician. Cosimo commissioned Ficino to translate the works of Plato—saying that he wanted Marsilio to turn from being a savior of bodies to being a savior of souls. Ficino also translated the works of Plotinus—completing the translation of these works in the same year that Columbus discovered America.

true, for example, in the case of Socrates. Through the ages various theories have been advanced as to which thinker has given the most accurate account of the philosophy of Socrates. As a consequence, Romero inclines to the view which paraphrases a Socratic dictum, i.e., that "with respect to Socrates, we know only that we know nothing."[33] However, Romero holds that Greek philosophy is very important to us not only because it is the origin of western philosophy but also because of the timeliness for our own day of the various insights of the great Greek sages.

Although time does doubtless obscure the contributions of earlier philosophers, Romero does not believe this to be always the case. He suggests that sometimes those who come after an innovator in philosophy see more in his new thought than he did himself. Thus "the creation of genius, the profound and prophetic intuition, the essential discovery are one thing; the consciousness and the exposition of all this, the worth and meaning assigned it are another. . . . There is no serious reason why a late expositor should not be more faithful to the ultimate significance and profound meaning of a thought than its author."[34]

But the fact that the personal equation enters into one's penetration into the thought of another should be kept in mind. That is, in accord with the Fichtean dictum, Romero remarks that the student of the history of philosophy sees it through his own ideas or even through "notions more lived than known, preferences, T-squares which we apply consciously or unconsciously."[35] Romero does not regard the realization of this fact as a cause for discouragement. He notes that Einstein denies that we have definite and exhaustive knowledge of the physical world yet states that each generation of investigators is bringing us nearer to such knowledge. Analogously, Romero thinks that those who delve into the theories of philosophers of the past are making progress toward a more adequate understanding of the significance of their insights. But these investigators must relive as well as rethink that past if they are to advance toward their goal. With Hegel began—Romero says—"the impassioned attempt to understand to its ultimate recesses the evolution of philosophical thought."[36] However, whereas Hegel put the history of philosophy on a sure course, he deformed his own contribution by his attempt to fit his historical insights into a fixed scheme. This mistake was avoided by Nicolai Hartmann, according to Romero, because his approach to the philosophy of the past was by way of "a free elaboration of problems."

Among the problems uncovered by a critical study of the history of philosophy is that of the relation between that history and the total history of man. This problem Romero regards as "one of the most far-reaching and grave." One question arising in this connection is concerned with just how much the original thinker contributes to the on-going of thought and how much he is helped to shape his new thought by the reaction on him of the climate of opinion in which he finds himself. Romero suggests that "each thinker receives and transmits an impulse whose direction helps to shape this historic curve."[37] One impulse which apparently helps to shape the direction of a genius's thought is the conception of the world entertained in a given epoch. This conception is a very important aspect of the climate of opinion in a given era. Naturally Romero recognizes the fact that one does not solve a problem simply by stating the questions which arise in connection with that problem—in this case the problem concerning what contribution an original thinker makes toward the development of man's understanding of himself and of the world around him. But for the solution of that problem these questions certainly must be brought out into the light. We can study the lives of great thinkers to see whether it seems true that the original thinker is influenced by his conceptual environment and in turn has an effect on it. If it is true that this is the case, a genius may fail to accomplish in a hostile environment what his great powers might have effected under more favorable circumstances. Thus Korn—as Romero points out—lived at a time when the person was devaluated so that he could not function adequately; could not achieve all that his noble capacities gave promise of performing.[38] Descartes, on the other hand, was the spokesman for his age.[39] He voiced the views latent in the minds of his contemporaries. A new day was dawning and he was the herald of that dawn—a real herald and not the chanticleer variety of herald. With that dawn the human being was emerging as important in his own right. Another case which might be recalled here is that of Heraclitus, whom Romero cites as ahead of his time and hence as misunderstood and unable to accomplish what he might have done in a time which was ripe for what he had in him to give; whereas "Hegel . . . was in many of his aspects a Heraclitus living again at a propitious time" and consequently could give an answer to the solicitations of his age. Hegel "arrived upon his hour as one arrives punctually for an appointment."[40] Again, Kant and Lambert anticipated the nebular theory of Laplace. Darwin was amazed to read in a manuscript of Alfred Russell Wallace a theory bearing some resemblance to his own. All these cases raise the question: how definitely can it be said that "new ideas originate in thoughts current in a period"?[41] Certainly the foregoing are some of the instances which might be adduced to show that the conception of the world or at least the climate of opinion at a given time seems to be one stimulus to a creative mind and one cause for the direction which the thought of that mind takes.

But what is the cause for a given world view? Romero fully recognizes the difficulty of answering his question. He suggests that one might assume that world views are "vast, unitary interpretations, universal formulae apparently justified at their appearance by plausible reasons, and they last until, by means of their very use, experience documents their limits and finally advises substitution." He likes this hypothesis because it implies "a critical use of experience and hence the consequent possibility of progressive approximation to the truth."[42] But this is only an hypothesis. He believes, however, that "ages have their own souls, their requirements, and even a sort of obscure program which they try to fulfill."[43] He cites the Cartesian enterprise as evidence that there is something in this supposition because Descartes "satisfied the capital demand of his time." As Descartes viewed the human being as autonomous in the area of knowledge so did the

ists, Descartes and Spinoza—did not break with the
his appreciation of the past on the part of Leibniz leads
to discuss man's rôle as an accumulator of the past.
connection, he states that "any loss in the past is a
loss for us all" and "any negligence and demeaning
past" means "depreciation and lack of recognition of
s."⁴⁹ This concern lest we forget what the past has
ted is most timely because, for example, there are
the recent past who turned their backs on the past
ed about "the wave of the future" as alone deserving
deration. This attitude became dangerously popular
to blindness concerning movements which claimed
w although they were only a covering for old ways
g disguised by new names—ways which enslaved
an liberated. Even today there seems to be, in some
a lack of comprehension of the significance of these
ts. Yet light from events in the past would dispel
and furnish one with a basis for genuine appraisal
movements.

ond idea advanced by Romero in discussing Leibniz
as follows: a failure to accomplish a significant pro-
later be seen in a different light—may even redound
lory. Specifically, Romero writes of Leibniz's dream
ng into existence an enlightened, harmonious com-
hat would be relieved of drudgery by means of
advances. He failed to bring about the fulfillment of
n as he had failed in some other projects. Even so,
makes this comment: "In historical perspective, the
between failure and success is not very clear, nor
ve great value."⁵⁰ This comment is one on which
do well to meditate, for human lives know so much
with no silver linings; of cherished purposes which
defeated; of fond hopes which have been shat-
newhere Barrie has put the matter this way: "The
ry man is a diary in which he means to write one
writes another; and his humblest hour is when he
he volume as it is with what he vowed to make it."
is well to think on the suggestion that from the

Reformation and the Natural Rights movement view him as autonomous in the religious and political fields. This example, Romero thinks, merely highlights the questions as to what gives rise to a world view; what part do the "great spirits of the time" play in originating and directing it? He does not think that the questions can be answered now.* Yet this can be said: that the human being, past ideas, and a given world view all play their parts in originating new ideas.⁴⁴

Before concluding this brief survey of a few of the points made by Romero in his philosophizing on the history of philosophy, it seems well to call attention to certain of the captivating items he has found in perusing the first histories of philosophy. Of course, as he states, some of these accounts are very valuable because of the information which they supply about various doctrines. Others are very intriguing. Thus Adam was said to be a mathematician because he could construct a house and make clothes for himself. He was said to be a physician because he could give animals names which fitted their natures. He was said to be a philosopher because, according to one account, he wrote some books—subsequently lost—but their titles were supposedly preserved. Cain was said to have sowed the first seeds of epicureanism. Another philosophical historian refers to a statement attributed to Eusebius, bishop of Caesarea in the fourth century, that Adam was a dialectician because he argued with Eve and the Serpent. Romero's comment here is that he is not sure that any history of dialectics has pointed out that Eve and the Serpent were more sucessful than Adam in argumentation.⁴⁵ An eighteenth century historian of philosophy re-

---

* Romero cites more points of interest than have been included here —as the reader will assume. He also has a very interesting discussion of the relation between a world view and a given method. Cf. Sobre la Historia de la Filosofía, pp. 79-88. It might be added that a contemporary artist has said that the new movements of today tend to be protests against earlier movements. The question as to what part is played by objections to earlier developments in art is an intriguing one. How helpful would it be to raise that question in connection with developments in other fields? Or is it like saying—to limit the suggestion to an individual case—that a certain prominent person would ride his horse facing backwards, if that could be done, because others face in the direction in which the horse is going?

garded the fall of Adam as evidence that he was a "deplorable philosopher" since he allowed himself to be persuaded "by gross arguments to violate the order of the Creator." In the seventeenth century there were discussions concerning the philosophical knowledge of angels and of devils. In the eighteenth century some historians of philosophy felt it necessary to deny the existence of antediluvian philosophy. Romero thinks it strange that they felt it necessary to take a position on this matter instead of simply ignoring it.[46]

So much for a few interesting items found in some seventeenth and eighteenth century histories of philosophy. It should be observed here that, although we have not mentioned the names of these historians, Romero has very carefully documented his discussion of them. However, our references to these earlier writers have been so brief that it has seemed best to omit names. Were names included, we should say something about their genuine contributions as Romero has done. There are two further points which should be made here. There was an attempt in philosophical historiography of the eighteenth century to include the views of all known peoples, even the Malabars, the Indians of Canada, and the Hyperboreans. Romero believes that—instead of criticizing these philosophical historians—it is of more moment to consider their intentions. In fact he thinks that such criticism might be cruel. Here again we have evidence of the fact that Romero is a great and generous thinker, for his desire is to understand the views of others rather than to proceed to judge those views from the standpoint of his own position. But, since he is a thinker, he naturally wishes to account, if possible, for the universalism of the eighteen century philosophical histories—or, to put the matter in his graphic way—to determine why the eighteenth century "set itself the task of registering all philosophy thought by men, sniffing in all corners of the Planet" so as to omit nothing.[47] He holds that the eighteenth century did this "sniffing in all corners" because of a "discolored rationalism compromised with empiricism." The rationalism was "discolored" due to the fact that the reasonable was assumed to be what is based on "a modicum of good sense." Furthermore rationalism was "tied too wide view—which has been said to be in itself a healing thing—perhaps the failure is not the crushing thing which it appears to be at the time. And it is indeed the business of one who seeks to achieve this wide view to strive to be "a spectator of all time and all existence" as Plato phrased that attitude. And who can afford not so to strive if one is to "make the most of his chance at life"? Such an attitude is the attitude of the person who "looks before and after" and yet does not "pine for what is not" but attempts to see from a high eminence in order to understand and hence to live in accordance with that enlightenment concerning what is of transcendent importance.

Before we turn from even this short reference to Romero's discussion of Leibniz, we should mention the fact that Romero believes the fame of Leibniz will increase when more of his voluminous writings have been published. And certainly the interest in various quarters in securing such publication supports Romero's view. In contrast to this concern to make available more of Leibniz's writings in order that he may be more fully comprehended and thus appreciated is the belief expressed by one writer concerning another German philosopher. This other writer believes that Heidegger would not be so highly regarded today if more than one volume of his *magnum opus* had been published. We should remember in the case of Heidegger the suggestion that one can not understand the reason for his existentialism unless one realizes that this theory was developed by him between the two world wars. If this is the reason for the central place which he has given to anguish, a reader of Heidegger can readily understand his difficulty in rising to any wider view of things as they are. In those darkest hours, what else could be expected of him? However the main tenets of his position emphasize the need for achieving a more elevated point of view in order to present a philosophy which rests on the love of wisdom and hence is more in tune with the main current of the historical development of philosophy.

In contrast to Heidegger's breaking away from the continuity of philosophical thought as it comes down to us from the past, Nicolai Hartmann has been able "to weave into his own woof" threads from both early and later philosophical investigation. As Romero has indicated, Hartmann has not been interested in discovering something new, hence his timeliness. His theory of value rests heavily on that of Schiller; his study of the irrational has been aided by Lask's research; indeed his thought depends on "the whole philosophical consciousness of the West." Romero goes on to say that, where contradictions have occurred in the history of philosophy, Hartmann believes that these are due to the "will to system" which has existed in the past. He does not believe that it is necessary to start with a preconceived idea—as system makers have done—in order to reach a "vision of the whole." Hartmann maintains that ultimately systematic thought can achieve such a vision even though the thinker is not attempting to fit that thought into a system. We shall have more to say concerning the position of Hartmann in Chapter I where we present Romero's problematic approach to philosophy. The reason for continuing this discussion of Hartmann is that Romero finds himself in sympathy with Hartmann's idea that the problematic rather than the systematic approach to philosophy is the more fruitful at this time. Furthermore Romero finds certain significant points in Hartmann's discussion on this topic.

As for the other chapters, the following points should be made. In Chapter II we shall consider briefly Romero's discussion of Cartesian reason. The next two chapters are an introduction to Romero's anthropological philosophy. In Chapter V we shall present cogent points in the central concept of his metaphysics: transcendence. Through transcendent activity culture is created and thus our next concern will be his ontology of culture. Finally we must remember that Romero thinks of philosophy as more than an academic discipline. Hence philosophy has something so say about problems arising in daily life as well as about ultimates. Today the fact of crisis presents a challenge to everyone and any light that Romero can throw on the causes and cure of crises will be welcome. He played an important part in resolving the crisis in Argentina. As a consequence anything that he has to say on the subject of crisis will be valuable. So much for a statement of the problems with which the subsequent chapters deal. It is a statement which makes quite clear that this exploration of Romero's thought is only an introduction to his very significant contributions to the clarification of a few of the many problems which he has taken under consideration.

REFERENCES AND NOTES

1. F. Romero, SOBRE LA FILOSOFIA EN AMERICA, Editorial Raigal, Buenos Aires, 1952, p. 18. Note also, in the same book, his implied astonishment that Borden Bowne's life was passed almost exclusively in study and teaching; that his biography "registers no other success worthy of being noted." p. 107.
2. This is a translation of a statement in an invitation to join ASCUA. *Cf.* the *boletín* containing ASCUA's "Declaración de Principios," Buenos Aires, 20 Junio 1952.
3. Romero was a member of Group A, a group composed of persons who are working in philosophy or in related fields.
4. For an account of the life of Romero see REVISTA CUBANA DE FILOSOFIA, Vol. II, Num. 9, pp. 5 ff.
5. Romero was once labelled a personalist by the late Edgar Brightman. But Romero—though mentioning that fact—very gently but very explicitly declines to comment on this designation in his discussion of those personalists who regarded Bowne as their founder. In view of his position on systems in general, it is reasonable to assume that Romero would prefer not to be classified. *Cf.* SOBRE LA FILOSOFIA EN AMERICA, pp. 110-111.
6. *Ibid.*, p. 11.
7. *Ibid.*, p. 22. *Cf.* also pp. 11-49.
8. *Ibid.*, p. 19.
9. F. Romero, FILOSOFIA DE LA PERSONA, Editorial Losada, S. A., Buenos Aires, 1944, p. 106.

10. *Cf.* SOBRE LA FILOSOFIA EN AMERICA, p. 44.
11. F. Romero, FILOSOFIA DE AYER Y DE HOY, Argos, Buenos Aires, 1947, p. 100.
12. *Cf. ibid.*, pp. 98 ff. The projected visit did not materialize.
13. *Cf.* F. Romero, ALEJANDRO KORN, Editorial Reconstruir, Buenos Aires, 1956, pp. 14 ff, and FILOSOFIA DE AYER Y DE HOY, pp. 236, 238, and 239.
14. ALEJANDRO KORN, p. 19.
15. *Cf.* ALEJANDRO KORN, pp. 26 and 47 and FILOSOFIA DE AYER Y DE HOY, pp. 237 and 239.
16. *Cf.* F. Romero, QUE ES LA FILOSOFIA, Editorial Columba, Buenos Aires, 1953, pp. 17-21.
17. *Ibid.*, p. 14.
18. *Cf. ibid.*, pp. 29-32.
19. *Ibid.*, p. 45.
20. SOBRE LA FILOSOFIA EN AMERICA, p. 110.
21. *Ibid.*, p. 111.
22. FILOSOFIA DE LA PERSONA, p. 20.
23. *IBID.*, pp. 27-28.
24. SOBRE LA FILOSOFIA EN AMERICA, p. 115.
25. FILOSOFIA DE LA PERSONA, pp. 24-25 and 31.
26. T. Mann, THE LIVING THOUGHTS OF SCHOPENHAUER, Longmans, Green, and Company, New York, 1939, p. 9.
27. *Cf.* SOBRE LA FILOSOFIA EN AMERICA, pp. 106 and 121.
28. *Ibid.*, p. 101.
29. *Ibid.*, p. 99.
30. FILOSOFIA DE AYER Y DE HOY, p. 7.
31. *Cf. ibid.*, pp. 8-9.
32. F. Romero, SOBRE LA HISTORIA DE LA FILOSOFIA, Universidad Nacional de Tucumán, Tucumán, 1943, p. 8.
33. *Ibid.*, p. 13, *Cf.* also pp. 14-17.
34. *Ibid.*, p. 18.
35. *Ibid.*, p. 21.
36. *Ibid.*, p. 22. *Cf.* also pp. 24-26.
37. *Ibid.*, p. 32

38. *Cf.* FILOSOFIA DE AYER Y DE HOY, pp. 236 ff.
39. *Cf.* F. Romero, ESTUDIOS DE HISTORIA DE LAS IDEAS, Editorial Losada, S. A., Buenos Aires, 1953, pp. 38-39.
40. SOBRE LA HISTORIA DE LA FILOSOFIA, p. 37.
41. *Ibid.*, p. 36. *Cf.* also p. 35.
42. *Ibid.*, p. 44.
43. *Ibid.*, p. 45.
44. *Cf. ibid.*, p. 45-46.
45. *Cf. ibid.*, p. 57.
46. *Cf. ibid.*, pp. 57-58.
47. *Ibid.*, p. 56.
48. *Cf. ibid.*, pp. 61-64.
49. FILOSOFIA DE AYER Y DE HOY, p. 12.
50. *Ibid.*, p. 28.

CHAPTER I

ON THE PROBLEMATIC APPROACH TO PHILOSOPHY

As we have already indicated in the "Introduction," Romero states that there are two philosophical attitudes: the systematic and the problematic. He believes that the age of system making has passed and that the philosopher's business is that of dealing with problems. He must not try to fit newly discovered data into the frame of a system constructed in an *a priori* fashion. Indeed, philosophy should proceed to make whatever contributions it can to the solution of problems without presuppositions which may lead to the disregard of important data and which may also result in the misinterpretation of the data before one. In philosophizing, then, one needs to know the facts and "to meditate on them without other preoccupation than that of the truth."[1] The difficulties in achieving such rigorous thinking are obviously many. They are, for example, "mental habits, previous individual and collective notions, preferences, aspirations, in a word all *idola* which intervene continuously to impress distortions on the progress of thought."[2]

Awareness of these difficulties is one safeguard in the business of solving problems. To more completely appreciate Romero's attitude on the problematic approach to philosophy we shall now consider some of his statements concerning Nicolai Hartmann. Romero holds that "Hartmann is not a discoverer of new directions. He does not delight in the rare find; he does not try to dazzle the reader nor to surprise him. ... His part seems to be to listen to the heart of the moment and to tell us how it beats. He lends his own voice to the philosophic consciousness of the age and attempts to tell us in express terms what . . . are its proposals or programs. . . . And this ability of his to coincide with the deeply secret and unanimous palpitation of the age does not show lack of originality . . . much less autonomous, laborious, and intense reflection. The brilliant sparkle of out-of-the-way ideas is easier; the frequenting of unused bypaths more pleasant. . . . Almost all of the essential themes developed by Hartmann have been investigated by other philosophers."[3] In other words, Hartmann has not attempted to be original, to present unique ideas, but he has made it his business "to continue the tasks of the centuries." He has done this in the way that his awareness of the needs of the time dictates. What Romero says of Hartmann could well be said of Romero's own concern. He too has a predilection for exploring problems, especially such problems as transcendence, structure, spirit, liberty, values, and culture.

At the same time he recognizes the fact that the making of systems came about as an answer to a felt need. He accounts for the earlier interest in system making by what he calls the "human inquietude before the great problems of all ages." Hence there is "urgency to give these problems an answer as quickly as possible"—an answer which will "remove and lessen our lack of tranquility before them."[4] These systems, then, were constructed to supply answers to these ultimate problems. Romero holds that today those who think rigorously "aspire to a vision of the whole," yet they do not accept an *a priori* schema as a guide for shaping their investigations. However systematic thought does tend toward a unified concept even though it does not presuppose such a concept, as did the classical systems. In the classical systems the plan of the system came first and the data were squeezed into this plan. As one consequence, important problems were omitted. Thus, for example, materialism eluded such problems as life and spirit, refusing to take these into account.[5]

In emphasizing his objection to system makers, Romero compares them to Cervantes' nobleman who, upon finding that he did not have a helmet, fashioned one out of cardboard. He tested the cardboard helmet but it did not stand the test. Hence he remade the helmet but put it to no further test because he had to have faith in the helmet. As a consequence he ran the risk of being defenceless before an enemy. Just so, those who put their trust in systems run the risk of "taking for finely tempered steel what in reality is only cardboard."[6] In other words, one should beware of taking as solutions of problems those conclusions which have not been carefully tested and thus have not been demonstrated as adequately accounting for the pertinent facts. Thus Romero points out the fallacy in adhering primarily to a system rather than to the facts which the system is supposed to bring together into a coherent whole. Certainly a system evolved before taking sufficient account of the facts does not give promise of being adequate. The failure to realize this is—Romero holds with Hartmann—a reason for the "surprising contradictions in the history of philosophy."

So much for indicating Romero's central reason for preferring the problematic approach to philosophy and his recognition of one rôle which systems have played. However, the problematic approach has its difficulties too and we turn to note briefly five cautions suggested by Romero. The most dangerous hindrance to philosophic work is the urgency which a thinker feels at times to arrive at answers to his problems.[7] The reason for this burning desire is that human life is short. The philosopher is not only a thinker "trying to elude all determinations of thought as one might attempt to leave behind his own shadow"; the philosopher is also a man with "a calendar and a watch," which measure the passage of time. These emphasize for him the brevity of his life and it is difficult for him to achieve "the primary virtue of the philosopher." This difficult virtue is that of "the austere submission to the problem just as it is given to us and the persistent exploration of it," thus sacrificing—if necessary—the "natural fruit" of this labor, i.e., the immediate solution of the problem. The philosopher must not yearn for solutions during his short life. He must be content to envisage centuries of investigation of some of the problems whose answers seem vital to him even though, as a man, he wishes an immediate solution for "peace of soul, tranquility, the comfortable bridge over the abyss, the calm siesta in the shade of a certainty."[8] As understandable as is this desire, man's need is to lift his sights and to be satisfied with what contribution he can make toward solutions even if he cannot supply final answers to certain problems.

Besides cautioning against a demand for ready answers to problems, Romero cites a supposition about problems—a supposition which he, with Hartmann, regards as erroneous. This assumption is that the philosopher should turn away from insoluble problems. Romero thinks that the history of philosophy shows progress in what he designates as "its battle with the highest enigmas." By these *enigmas* he means such problems as substance, liberty, reality, and life. Romero believes that the history of philosophy shows that meditation on these problems by successive thinkers has illumined these enigmas. Furthermore, the unsolved problem beckons thought onward whereas a problem solved closes the road ahead.* Indeed "the valuable, the permanent in the treasury of the history of philosophy is the indefatigable investigation of problems such as they are given to us, in their completely problematic character, without subordinating them to the recompense, the prize that is the satisfaction of our metaphysical need."[9] That is, the exploration of the problem is the important contribution which any one thinker can make. This is his function with regard to the "highest enigmas."

Again, there is the assumption that man raises problems;

---

* This statement about the closed road in the case of the problem solved and the beckoning onward of the difficult problem reminds one of a section of a paper read by Whitehead about thirty years ago. In this section Whitehead stressed the fact that, after the winning of a cause, the winners may rest their oars, so to speak. As a consequence, the accomplishment falls short of what might have been achieved. On the other hand, there is a vitality about lost causes which the cause that is won often does not exhibit. While the analogy between the thought of Romero and that of Whitehead is not close, Whitehead's point is of such significance that I have chosen to mention it, though the excuse for so doing is slight.

that, if they were not formulated by man, these problems would not arise. This is an error, Romero points out, for problems present themselves to man as do the physical objects of his environment. It is of course true that the context in which a problem arises does influence the form in which the problem presents itself. But the problem itself is the same problem, seen each time in a different light. The problems which he has in mind here are enigmas which have always existed, even though they may not have appeared as questions until "a certain level of philosophic consciousness has been reached."[10]

The fourth caution is to proceed methodically, as Hartmann has pointed out. The very important first stage is the careful investigation of facts. But this is only the first stage rather than the only one, as appears to be the case in Husserl's thought. The second stage is the analysis of the problem—a stage important to Aristotle. Here one determines what is problematic in the data, what must be scrutinized ever so carefully in order to be able to advance an answer, if an answer is possible. This answer is the third stage.[11]

There is a still further caution, noted by Romero, closely linked with this one. It is not a caution which Romero discusses in connection with Hartmann's problematic approach, however. This caution is against a method-ridden procedure. In other words, one must not allow method to dominate research any more than system, and yet there has been such domination. Thus the rationalists who pursued the geometrical method presented by Descartes seemed to think that, "an intelligence that, for a given moment, should know all the forces animating nature and the respective situations of all beings that compose it," such an intelligence could calculate past and future events.[12] In other words, to use Du-Bois Reymond's example, it was assumed that "one could conclude who the Man in the Iron Mask was as well as the moment in which England would burn its last piece of coal." That is, the assumption of these rationalists was that reality is a logical order which pure reason can know. Their method originated from this theory and into the frame of this method facts were expected to fit. If such was not the case, either the misfit was not noticed or the assumption was that at a later time the difficulties would be overcome and then the facts would fit. The method itself was regarded as being what Caesar's wife should always be, i.e., above suspicion. The empiricists, on the other hand, viewed reality only as the immediately given and consequently ignored the fact that some entities are "foreign to temporality." Their method originated from this world view. They attempted to force facts into the frame of the empirical method. They did not detect the deforming of certain facts as a result of this procedure. In general, fortunately, methods which were regarded as so correct that facts must be retouched to fit the given method did not eliminate all difficulties. Eventually—as Romero graphically puts it—the promissory notes were presented for payment.[13] Only then was the method seen as bankrupt.*

So much for cautions in connection with the problematic approach to philosophy. Of course these cautions could be applied to work in philosophy in general, as Romero indicates. Our next concern is with two other points: one, the antiquity of the problematic approach, and, two, the necessity that philosophy keep in touch with the problems of the day. First, then, the problematic approach is not a new one. Romero refers to Hartmann's belief that both the constructive and the problematic approaches have been present

---

* Writing in the same vein in 1939 Romero discussed the Nazi program and its disastrous conjunction with a theory not adequately established. He stated that a theory about reality is only an hypothesis and needs correction in the light of new findings. Theories about human beings are much more liable to error than those about the physical world and much more liable to be twisted in accord with subjective desire. When a theory is made a part of a practical program for attaining a desired end, the chance for its correction in the light of new facts is gone. "The theoretical pretension and supposed necessary derivation of the practical consequences elude the confrontation with the elemental principles which should rule conduct. . . . All appears justified and necessary. . . . Irresponsibility is encouraged." "While the theorizations on a war footing . . . menace the world, a mental chaos threatens in its turn those who support these theories." Romero goes on to write of our condemnation of this policy of confusion and violence and of the fact that this policy will throw obscuration and disorder into the souls of those who pursue it. *Cf.* FILOSOFOS Y PROBLEMAS, Editorial Losada, S. A., Buenos Aires, 1947, pp. 161-171.

throughout the development of philosophic thought. Sometimes a given thinker has made first one approach and then the other. Plato, Aristotle, Descartes, Hume, Leibniz, and Kant are cited as thinkers who—though system makers—were predominately investigators of problems. Because their main concern was not to achieve a system, their work has had more lasting significance. The exploring of problems in the past has amounted to more than the making of systems.[14]

As for problems of the present day, Romero believes very deeply that the philosopher must be alert to the vital issues of his day. We have referred to his work as a member of the *Comisión Organizadora de ASCUA*.* The members of *ASCUA* were professors and students, persons in other professions, business men and workers. Their stated goal was to oppose a campaign which began with the purpose of obscuring the tradition of May—a campaign which thus sought to confuse appreciation of the events attending the origin of the nation.[15] The members of *ASCUA* saw in that tradition "a profound movement of emancipation . . . having as its aim the establishment of a humanistic democracy."[16] To achieve their purpose these men organized seminars, courses, conferences, and issued publications in order to bring together men from all walks of life. Romero's work with *ASCUA* is only one of his many contributions toward the solution of his country's problems. Hence Risieri Frondizi has said that one notices in Romero qualities which show that he is indeed a great and generous man, who feels responsible for the future of his country as well as for that of all Latin America.**

One indication of Romero's feeling of responsibility has just been presented in this sketchy statement of main points in his view concerning the problematic approach to philosophy. We have noted something of the advantages of this approach, the cautions to be observed, its antiquity, and the desire of the Latin American thinker to gain first hand

---

* *Cf.* "Introduction."
** *Cf.* PHILOSOPHY AND PHENOMENOLOGICAL RESEARCH, Vol. IX, No. 2, p. 338.

knowledge of problems rather than to lead an ivory tower-like existence. Since the presentation has been so fragmentary, certain comments are in place. While the outstanding advantage of this approach is that data do not have to be fitted into a preconceived scheme, there is the question which a person, remembering Auguste Comte, might raise. The question is this: can one observe without a theory? A fuller discussion of Romero's view would make clear that his objection is not to an hypothesis which is developed as one's exploration goes on. Romero's objection is to an *a priori* construction which is so strictly adhered to that sometimes *the given* which is being investigated has to be deformed in order that it may be included in the system, while other data are even denied the status of *the given*.

As for Romero's warning against ill-advised haste in seeking answers to problems, one is reminded of Omar Kháyyám's would-be unraveler of "the master knot of human fate." No more graphic picture could be painted of the disastrous consequences of such impatience. The youth who briefly turned to the wise to be told *all* did not possess what Romero regards as "the primary virtue of the philosopher." This young man was not willing to search diligently for the key to that door for which he found no key at once; he was not prepared to labor arduously to pierce that veil through which he could not see quickly. He could not have retired sooner than he did from hearing "some little talk awhile of me and thee" if he had suddenly become acquainted with Heraclitus' assumption that truth is hidden, not by one veil, but by a hundred veils. The impetuous explorer tried to satisfy his quest for certainty hastily and eventually arrived at three kinds of pessimism. Moreover, in the end, his paradise became a desert, where he, a thirsting traveler, yearned for a fountain even if dimly revealed; the angel for whom he longed was not "thou beside me singing" but a winged one, powerful enough to "make the stern Recorder otherwise enregister, or quite obliterate." The only immortality he envisioned was that he live long enough in the memory of a certain friend for that friend to "turn down an empty glass" for him where he had formerly engaged in festivities. He never learned that life should be moulded not "nearer to the heart's desire but to the soul's."

Omar Kháyyám's impatient seeker found that, in his case, the urgent attempt to solve problems quickly brought new problems. Indeed it is proverbial that "haste makes waste." Obviously Romero did not intend to say that man has nothing to do with creating some problems for himself. But the problems which Romero has in mind are the genuinely philosophical problems, which have always existed but appear only when a "certain stage or level of philosophical consciousness" has been attained. He has guarded his statement adequately for his reference is to the "highest enigmas." We might introduce as an example of his thought the question concerning the nature of beauty. This would be a problem whether or no it ever occurred to man to raise the inquiry as to the nature of beauty. Here we might recall that Plato, as a writer of schoolboy lyrics, was not interested in the aesthetic problem concerning the nature of beauty. It was enough for him that the passionate desire to express intense feeling found outlet in satisfying form. It was enough for him that the turbulence in his young heart was eased by objectifying his emotion in poetry that induced harmony in the innermost places of his soul. But the love of his adolescent years—the artist's love for creation—gradually gave place to the philosophic urge to know the essence of beauty's being. This latter urge was nourished by the teachings of Socrates. Plato came to realize that beauty is different from beautiful things but he was in a quandary at first about the distinctive nature of beauty. This problem was not one thought up by Socrates; it was not, as it were, a spiderlike web spun out of his own mental processes. But this problem presented itself as truly to the mind of the thinker as did Phidias' *Athena* present itself to his eyes. This sort of thing, I take it, is what Romero means in stating that problems will arise whether man asks questions or not. And it is Romero's way of answering those who scoff at the philosopher's quest, or so it seems to me.

As for Romero's designating certain philosophical problems as enigmas—as insoluble—he might have run the risk of implying more knowledge of them than he professes. That is, to know that a problem is insoluble would mean that one knows enough about it so that he can claim that it is beyond the limits of human intelligence. Locke, in stating that the *substratum* is unknowable, committed this fallacy. But Romero's discussion of insoluble problems indicates that he is using the term in the historical sense rather than in the absolute sense. For example, the nature of life, which he mentions as one of the problems, is not completely known. Thus, for example, we know a great deal about the nucleus of the protoplasmic cell which is the beginning of man. We know things about biological life. We also know things about abundant life and at times sympathize with the logical positivist's position when he relegates questions about what constitutes the abundant life to the limbo of pseudo questions. But these questions have enduring significance for us, the living, and we can not shrug them off by classifying them as pseudo. However, we may be certain that so great a thinker as Romero would not care to become prophetic concerning the eventual possibility, if there is a possibility, of solving such a problem as that concerning the nature of life. His discussion of method, for example, exhibits his reluctance to make any pronouncement except on the basis of sufficient data.

REFERENCES

1. F. Romero, FILOSOFOS Y PROBLEMAS, Editorial Losada, S. A. Buenos Aires, 1947, p. 161.
2. *Ibid.*, p. 161.
3. F. Romero, FILOSOFIA CONTEMPORANEA, Editorial Losada, S. A., Buenos Aires, 1944, pp. 10-11.
4. *Ibid.*, p. 13.
5. *Cf. ibid.*, pp. 14-15.
6. *Ibid.*, p. 17.
7. *Cf. ibid.*, pp. 19-20.
8. *Ibid.*, p. 18.
9. *Ibid.*, pp. 21-22.
10. *Ibid.*, p. 22.

11. *Cf. ibid.*, p. 23-24.
12. *Cf.* SOBRE LA HISTORIA DE LA FILOSOFIA, p. 82.
13. *Cf. ibid.*, pp. 82-86.
14. *Cf.* FILOSOFIA CONTEMPORANEA, p. 16.
15. *Cf. boletín* containing statement of reason for creating *ASCUA* and "Declaración de Principios," Buenos Aires, 20 junio 1952, p. 1.
16. *Ibid.*, p. 1.

Chapter II

CARTESIAN REASON

As we stated in the preceding chapter, Romero is interested in the exploration of problems of philosophy rather than in the development of a philosophical system. One of the problems which concerns him is that of the nature of reason and it is a very urgent problem not only for the student of the history of philosophy but also for the thinker anxious to throw light on certain, pressing and perplexing problems of today, especially as there is a contemporary tendency to debunk reason, to declare it unfitted for the task of charting a course of human thought and action. Romero has called attention to the different meanings which reason has had in the minds of those using the term during the long history of human thought. It has seemed best to limit this discussion to pertinent points in Romero's examination of Cartesian reason and to a brief exposition of his view that intelligence is a wider concept than reason.

First, then, concerning the rationalism of Descartes, Romero compares his message with that of Spinoza and Leibniz. He says that these men are the three greatest rationalists of the modern age but that they had messages which were significant for different areas of time: Spinoza had a message for all time; Leibniz had a message for the future; while Descartes had a message for his own time.[1] In fact, Romero thinks that a great merit of the Cartesian philosophy was that it satisfied the demands of the seventeenth century. In the first place, it was exactly the rationalism which the age required and hence was in tune with other developments of the century. For example, Descartes' theory of substance and of the external world harmonized with the thought of Galileo.[2] In the second place, Descartes' views were not such that they broke sharply with traditional theories. For example, Descartes dualism was analagous to the Christian view that body and soul are distinct.[3] It is Romero's considered opinion that, with Descartes, philosophy came of age. Whereas Renaissance thought was an adolescent type of philosophy since it was a mixture of poetry and philosophy, Descartes brought about "the establishment of a firm beginning for philosophy." Romero even wonders what the fate of philosophical development would have been without Descartes, for he "was able to elude the risks of the historical occasion and to guide the ship of free philosophy between the most dangerous reefs."[4]*

Before embarking on a detailed examination of Romero's view concerning Cartesian reason, we must first note Romero's emphasis on the difficulty of answering the primary question about the nature of reason. Romero likens the difficulty of answering this question to the difficulty mentioned by St. Augustine when he was asked to state the nature of time. It was easy enough for him to know the nature of time if he was not asked for a statement about it; but, when asked, he realized his ignorance. Romero thinks that the same might be said with regard to reason. It seems to him that the attitude of the seventeenth century toward reason supports his contention that it is difficult to state the nature of reason. The seventeenth century, Romero says, accepted reason as a faith and did not investigate it. The knowledge which we have of the nature of reason—and this is little enough—is knowledge gained from the adversaries of reason. Conse-

---

* Romero very graphically suggests the possibility that, were it not for Descartes, "modern philosophy would have been very different from what it was: it would have been a beautiful body without a head, like the Victory of Samothrace, but without continuing to be, as that is, even decapitated, a Victory." ESTUDIOS DE HISTORIA DE LAS IDEAS, Editorial Losada, S. A., Buenos Aires, 1953, p. 62.

quently a true estimate of rationalism has still to be made.[5]

Although such an appraisal is still lacking, Romero believes that reason has "very solid and true virtues." Some insight concerning what those virtues are will be gained by considering what Romero regards as two important defects of Cartesian reason. One defect is that it is immanent rather than transcendent.[6] First we shall attempt to make clear what Romero means by this criticism and in doing so we shall see why he objects to reason that is immanent. Secondly we shall notice the basis of this claim of immanence. As for the objection to reason that is immanent, the point is this. In the case of such reason the individual looks within, whereas the opposite rightly transpires. That is, the attention is directed outward—the knower sinks himself in the object and lets the object reveal itself to him. In so doing, the knower achieves an insight that is objective and universal rather than subjective.[7]

Why does Romero regard Cartesian reason as immanent? One basis for this opinion is to be found apparently in the sixth of the MEDITATIONS. The reason for so assuming is that Romero believes that Descartes expounded his view of reason chiefly in his examinaton of corporeal reality.[8] Let us recall the special passages which Romero seems to have in mind. Descartes asserted that formerly he based his thinking on sense perception. Then he discovered his errors in judgment. As a consequence it seemed reasonable to conclude that corporeal things are not just what the senses show them to be. Indeed comprehension by the senses is often "obscure and confused." Those things, however, which are conceived "clearly and distinctly"—those things which are the object of pure mathematics—are really known. In this activity of knowing, the mind "in some manner turns on itself," the mind examines the ideas which it finds in its storehouse. Through this introspective procedure the mind can gain a comprehension of external objects more adequately than it was able to do through sense perception.[9] This turning of the attention inward is the procedure to which Romero objects. He regards this procedure as immanentization rather than transcendence. Yet transcendence is necessary if one is to gain insight into corporeal reality, from Romero's standpoint.

Another basis for Romero's contention that Cartesian reason is immanent is to be found in the Cartesian view of substance—a view which Romero regards as formed because of the principle of identity. What is meant here needs further elucidation. Romero claims that immanentism and rationalism coincide. He says that the first principle of Cartesian reason is identity. This principle, as Romero sees it, expresses mere identity rather than a necessary condition of change—i.e., that throughout change something persists, else there would not be change but chaos. Romero believes that the principle of mere identity is based on ontological identity. He maintains that the notion of classical substance was developed partly because of the requrement of identity. This principle, that A is A and nothing but A, affirms immanence, for transcendence would take A beyond itself to something other than itself. Romero regards himself as at one with Hegel on this point, since Hegel's logic was a logic of becoming and hence a logic of transcendence rather than a logic which accepts the principle of identity.[10]

In short, Romero's view of Cartesian reason is that it introspects in order to reach the true. Furthermore, in this process reason arrives at a concept of matter such that matter is viewed as bare identity, as that which has not within itself the possibility of becoming.

Turning now to the second criticism of Cartesian reason, we find Romero objecting to clarity as a demand of reason. Before dealing with this demand of Descartes, Romero notes that the first philosophers chose transparent bodies—water and air—as worthy of being regarded as substances. Then Parmenides gave a statement of *being* which is reducible to a list of negations—a list which anticipates Descartes' famous discussion of a piece of wax. Thus reason has been prone to construe being mathematically. Reason does this in order to subtract the opaque and thus to feel that it attains full knowledge.[11] However, reason errs, for all is not *sonnenklar* and the assumption that one can arrive at such clarity is false.

But elsewhere it is a merit of Descartes, Romero points

out, to realize that reason has its limitations.* Thus, while Romero regards Descartes' grasp of the nature of reason as defective in the two respects which we have discussed, Romero does call attention to this insight of Descartes. The special limitation to which Romero calls attention is the need of reason for the aid of the will if truth is to be attained. Reason needs this aid if it is to discard "convictions fortified by custom, the deceits of ordinary perception, and the usual belief in what we know or imagine we know by tradition or experiences which life affords us." It is obvious, then, that "the Cartesian intellectualism is accompanied by voluntarism": by a "will to truth," so essential if truth is to be attained.[12] Of course Descartes recognizes that the will has been accustomed to act on incomplete knowledge and consequently needs to school itself to wait until the evidence is in before proceeding to act. Romero compares such renunciation to the act of an heir to a fortune who chooses to give it up and also to give up advantages that might accrue to him because of his fortune, i.e., social position and friendships. This choice is made because the heir desires to win for himself money and these other advantages without being beholden to anyone.[13]

Up to this point we have indicated that Romero finds both defect and merit in Descartes' view of reason. But the merit outweighs the defect for "to place in the depths of the individual, of the person; to recognize that his will is necessary to assert it, Descartes, at the beginning of modern

---

* We might recall here for ourselves particular passages in which Descartes emphasized the limitations of reason. Thus, in his RULES FOR THE DIRECTION OF THE MIND, Rule VIII states that there are problems which the human intelligence cannot solve. In his preface to the Reader, which serves as an introduction to his MEDITATIONS, Descartes maintained that the Deity cannot be known completely by the human mind. Furthermore, in MEDITATION IV, Descartes mentioned his inability to understand the dealings of the Deity with man but expressed the belief that there is no reason why God should make His ways clear to His child. Descartes observed that an "infinity of things" escapes man's comprehension. In these passages the word for reason has not occurred but it will be recalled that, in his answer to the third set of objections to his MEDITATIONS, Descartes used several words as synonyms for reason and even included feeling among thinking activities.

philosophy made a generous allegation in the epistemological field comparable to that which at the end of the era Immanuel Kant made on the ethical plane."[14] That is, Descartes emphasized the supreme importance of each man as a free, responsible being, as a repository of truth, in so far as human beings are capable of such attainment.

The merit of Cartesianism was obvious to those thinkers who, however, strove to attain what they regarded as a more adequate view of reason. They made a sharp distinction between reason and feeling because they felt that feeling would blind one. Romero speaks of this eighteenth century rationalism as the rationalism of the seventeenth century generalized and vulgarized.[15] The *reason* of the eighteenth century philosophers was used to judge rather than to understand and reason held too closely to the dominant concepts, which were inadequate because they were developed by those who did not understand history.[16] Hence reason came to seem narrow and superficial. The consequence is, according to Romero, that we now view reason in this light and pass over its "very solid and true virtues."

The reaction against this "one-eyed reason," as Whitehead once labelled it, came in the form of Romanticism. After Rousseau left the fold of his former colleagues, the Encyclopaedists, he once exclaimed that they would as soon ascribe feeling to a stone as to a man. Like the Renaissance, Romanticism was a period of transition rather than a great epoch, Romero thinks. According to him, a great epoch is characterized by "the realization of a vast program and the application on a gigantic scale of a method." Furthermore this program and this method have persisted until they have lost their efficacy for "interpreting reality and for human conduct."[17] These marks of a great epoch were lacking in the Romantic era which was a period disseminating a "tumult of new intuitions," a period which had a predilection for the "vague and the obscure" as against the clear and the distinct. It recognized the importance, however, of those attributes on which rationalism had cast a jaundiced eye: "instinct, intuition, fantasy, feeling."[18] As a result, Romanticism was more concerned with religion and art than rationalism had been. Furthermore,

Romanticism fostered an interest in history. As a result, Romero points out, the interpretation of man has taken into account his "historical dimension." Since Romanticism was a period of rebellion, it naturally gave way to a new movement and yet "there is no essential theme of philosophy today which has not been made fruitful by a romantic seed."[19] Thus the defects of the rationalism succeeding Cartesianism instigated a movement which was very important for the development of human thought.

Yet there is an especial need now for a more adequate understanding of those "very solid and true virtues" of reason to which Romero refers for this age has been characterized as an age of retreat from reason. But throughout the modern period—as indeed earlier too—the reason of some men has impugned itself, the judge has also been the judged without, seemingly, a realization of this anomaly or the awareness that reason can not set limits to its power without already being beyond such limits, as Hegel saw. Because of the condemnation of reason by certain persons, those who have trusted reason have adopted various procedures. For example, some thinkers have tried to keep reason close to the "footpaths of earth" in order to prevent reason from going beyond its obvious data. Because this has been done, reason's findings have been characterized as "a torch of smoky pine," capable only briefly of illuminating the path into the future. These critics have made appeal to another capacity, variously named, in order to transcend the bounds which they have set to the insights of reason. Again, other thinkers who have trusted reason have attempted to lift its sights in order for it to fulfill its proper function. These thinkers have sought to raise their thought above the embroilments of daily life in order to understand the world in which we live. Their critics have accused them of indulging in whimsical notions which imply that reason is unwilling to roll up its sleeves and go to work in what sometimes really are eddies of "purposeless dust" rather than eddies which these critics regard as necessary accompaniments of facing facts.

As for Romero, he has taken full account of the shifting meanings given to reason in the past and has very wisely chosen to use the term *inteligencia* rather than the term *razón* to indicate intellectual activity. He has analyzed intelligence as follows: intelligence opens itself to objectifications "as much to indicate and to register them for cognitive purposes as to project and to create new syntheses for practical designs."[20] Romero goes on to say that intelligence seeks out empirical data and also attempts to discover the essence of reality. He regards intelligence so described as, "in a certain sense, above what is usually called 'reason' " or as wider than the concept of reason.[21] Although he does not attempt at this point a characterization of reason, he says: "Perhaps we might hazard the thought that by reason is understood a certain ideal order implanted in the field of intelligence, a rigid system of frames or norms which constrict the intelligence" by setting a pattern for it to follow.[22] Thus "reason is an ideal" and as such "has been conceived of in many ways." Hence reason can not be given a "single definition." On the other hand, "intelligence is an effective function, a fact; . . . defined above all by its acceptance of the objective order, by its capacity to submit itself to that which is. . . . It is the intelligence that has, throughout the march of philosophic thought constructed . . . various images of reason—images of itself in its desired perfection and purity—and it is likewise the intelligence that has confronted the contradictory enigmas of irrationality."[23] In other words, intelligence transcends private interests of the self in order to comprehend the objective order. Intelligence seeks to make of itself the knower as completely as it is possible for man to achieve this goal and thus, in its concept of reason, has outlined such perfection.

By coming to terms with the differing connotations of reason, Romero has wisely seen the advantage of using the term *inteligencia* to signify intellectual activity. Furthermore he has recognized the need for so-called irrational aids if one is really to understand. Thus one has to have sympathy with another—as James so graphically indicated in his Jack and Jill example—if one is genuinely to know that other. But Romero has also noted that, whereas there is today a more adequate appreciation of the irrational, there was in recent times "morbid delight" in the irrational on the part of well known thinkers; but this attitude is now corrected.[24]

Besides the necessity on the part of the intelligent person to appreciate the place of the irrational, there is also the necessity to understand differences in intelligent behavior and Romero offers this explanation. "The difference in intelligent behavior in one sphere or another is exterior to the intelligence itself and depends on the use to which it is applied, the purposes and ends toward which it is orientated. Subordinated to subjective particularism, the intelligence remains nailed to natural territory; emancipated, it turns to tasks of free knowledge, it becomes one of the faces of the spirit. . . . If, in its natural use, the intelligence does not reach beyond the limits of practical interest it is because it is found to be tied to subjective requirements. Freed of these requirements, it projects itself toward totality, in an enterprise seeking complete and unlimited knowledge."[25] In other words intelligence has both the function of fulfilling practical demands and the function of achieving absolute transcendence. In the exercise of this latter function, intelligence "can fulfill the most elevated cognitive functions."[26]

Such a brief discussion of intelligence as that presented here is only preliminary to a consideration of main points in Romero's anthropological philosophy and to those we now turn.

REFERENCES AND NOTES

1. *Cf.* ESTUDIOS DE HISTORIA DE LAS IDEAS, Editorial Losada, S. A., Buenos Aires, 1953, p. 38.
2. *Cf. ibid.*, p. 60.
3. *Cf. ibid.*, p. 61.
4. *Ibid.*, p. 63.
5. *Cf.* FILOSOFIA DE AYER Y DE HOY, Biblioteca Argos, Buenos Aires, 1947, pp. 31 and 35.
6. This, of course, is a position similar to that of Hegel.
7. *Cf.* PAPELES PARA UNA FILOSOFIA, Editorial Losada, Buenos Aires, 1945, p. 21. Romero writes of the Reformation as immanentization of faith; he refers to the

natural rights doctrine as the immanentization of sovereignty. Elsewhere he refers more approvingly to Descartes' signal contribution in his "revindication of the individual," since he postulated the individual as the "seat of knowledge." In so doing Descartes seems to Romero to have given voice to the demands of his time and to have uttered views held in common with others rather than merely private views. (*Cf.* SOBRE LA HISTORIA DE LA FILOSOFIA, Universidad de Tucumán, Facultad de Filosofía y Letras, Tucumán, 1943, p. 45.)

8. *Cf.* FILOSOFIA CONTEMPORANEA, Editorial Losada, S. A., Buenos Aires, 1944, p. 109 footnote.
9. *Cf.* Descartes, SELECTIONS, Charles Scribner's Sons, 1927, p. 147.
10. *Cf.* PAPELES PARA UNA FILOSOFIA, pp. 22-23. The reference to classical substance is clarified elsewhere by the statement that the judgment "Every body is extended" is an analytical judgment and hence falls under the principle of identity (LOGICA, p. 30). In connection with the reference to Hegel's view of identity we must recall Hegel's discussion of true identity.
11. *Cf. ibid.*, p. 104 and footnote, pp. 104-105.
12. ESTUDIOS DE HISTORIA DE LAS IDEAS, p. 50.
13. *Cf. ibid.*, p. 51.
14. *Ibid.*, p. 57.
15. *Cf.* FILOSOFIA DE LA PERSONA, Editorial Losada, S. A., Buenos Aires, 1944, p. 109.
16. *Cf. ibid.*, pp. 108-110.
17. PAPELES PARA UNA FILOSOFIA, p. 124.
18. *Ibid.*, p. 125.
19. *Ibid.*, p. 127.
20. TEORIA DEL HOMBRE, p. 72.
21. *Cf. ibid.*, pp. 73 and 228.
22. *Ibid.*, p. 228.
23. *Ibid.*, p. 73.
24. *Cf. ibid.*, p. 229.
25. *Ibid.*, p. 230.
26, *Ibid.*, p. 230.

CHAPTER III

ON MINIMAL MAN

We have been exploring Romero's theory concerning the nature of reason but to understand the man who reasons we obviously need light on other aspects of his nature and that light Romero has provided in his discussion of anthropological philosophy. Hence we present an introductory consideration of that philosophy.

Romero is of course fully aware of the impossibility of adequately knowing the nature of prehistoric man but finds it possible to make certain reliable inferences about the nature of early man on the basis of what we know of man when he appears at the dawn of history. In the first place, Romero holds that, in all life, *psyche* is present from the beginning but in animals *psyche* is not so fully developed as in man. Thus minimal man "is an intentional consciousness; without it he would not be man."[1] Romero very wisely does not attempt to explain the arrival of intentional consciousness or, better, the process by which *psyche* developed into intentional consciousness but notes simply that this event did take place and is "one of the most important facts in the history of the cosmos."[2] The animal, on the other hand, "lives blindly his psycho-organic states" and only in the superior animal is there sometimes evidence of a rudimentary intentional consciousness.

What are the primary features of intentional consciousness, according to Romero? "The essential characteristic of intentional consciousness is to consist in a bundle of intentions or acts projected toward objects."³ Romero goes on to say that man does have "states" which lack intentionality and that this is the case with animals. Animals *are* their "states" and such is the case of the human being at times—for example, when he is in great pain. Man is then that pain. As soon, however, as he knows the experience as pain, it is no longer a "state" but an object and he is a subject experiencing that pain, having that "state." Furthermore, the pain—now known as object—may be a stimulus for an intentional act. Thus the man who knows he is in pain may proceed to do something to alleviate the pain. Here, then, we have three steps: man knowing himself as the experiencer of pain, the pain as object, and the pain as stimulus to act in order to remove the pain.

Furthermore, minimal man, in possession of intentional consciousness, knows himself as subject—he is conscious of a self.* Also he perceives objects set over against this subject—"separate entities, endowed with existence and consistency of their own."⁴ Since this is Romero's view, he is not in agreement with those mystics who claim that there is a kind of knowledge in which there is no separation of subject and object—a separation which Romero regards as the *sine qua non* of the intentional consciousness. Moreover Romero does not understand how one can claim to possess a form of knowledge unless, at the same time, he perceives it as such, unless he is aware of it as something distinct from himself. The situation of this mystic seems to Romero very like that of a man who collects booty on a dark night. However he does not know what he has unless he brings the booty into the light and evaluates it. Likewise even intuitive knowledge to be grasped as insight must be in some sense objective to the man who possesses it. Hence even for the mystic, Romero believes that there exists the consciousness of objects as distinct from the self.⁵

---

* It will be remembered that Fichte thought that his little son had not developed the ability to think of himself as subject until he first said "Ich." When that occurred, Fichte gave a party to celebrate his child's coming to self consciousness.

Not only is intentionality characterized by the ability to recognize oneself as subject existing in a world of objects, but intentionality is also characterized by the ability to name, to communicate, and to judge. The ability to name and to communicate enables man "to be the heir and beneficiary of the conquests of the group."[6] This last point we would do well to ponder together with Edmund Burke's statement to the effect that we are "life-renters" and hence have the responsibility of being beneficiaries of those who follow us. To elaborate this point here is unnecessary because each person can more profitably think through the significance of these statements as they relate to his own sphere of activity.

In connection with naming as of prime importance in communicating, it is appropriate to dwell on man's ability to arrive at objectifications which have a universal reach—an ability which goes hand in hand with naming. This type of objectification is designated by Romero as a third type of objectification—the first being the recognition of something external to one as an object and the second being the noting of characteristics of that object. Thus I see the object before me as "pure object"* and then I observe that it has a certain shape and a particular color. The third type of objectification involves a synthesis of the common characteristics of objects before me. Through this synthesis I arrive at a general concept. All these objectifications require naming and this naming and these objectifications are fundamental to the advance of thought.[7] It will be remembered that James too has pointed out that primitive man had not at first developed his ability to reach certain abstract concepts. He would say, for example: "The face is a moon" or "the fruit is sugar cane" because the concepts of sweetness and roundness had not yet become explicit in his consciousness. Very little thought will convince one that these general concepts—these "objective signs" as Romero calls them—are essential to the advance of intelligent thinking.

Again, as for judging, Romero does not have in mind here

---

* *Pure object* is in this case a pen but *pen* is a general concept arrived at by means of the third type of objectification.

logical judgment but objectifying judgment: that is, this latter type of judgment is not focused on an object—as is logical judgment—but upon a state, which is objectified by such focusing. In advancing this view of objectifying judgment, Romero quotes Wundt, Witasek, Binet, and seventeen others who have recorded their opinions that, even in an act of perception, judgment enters in. Yet, while they are concerned with the act of perception and the function of judgment in relation to that act, Romero's view attributes a wider scope to the act of judging. He holds that "all objective presentation is constituted as such by a judicative act, whether it be an internal or an external perception, . . . an idea, a concept, a conclusion, something imaginary, etc., etc."[8] He further states that some thinkers would object to this position because they would conclude that it seems to make of reality a construct of perception, whereas they—in order to make clear that reality is independent of perception—think of the real as producing perceptions in our consciousness much—we might suggest—as we impress on the mirror a reflection of ourselves as we stand before the mirror. But Romero does not regard his view of perception as indicating at all that reality is a construction of the judgment which enters into perception. He states that the reality perceived "is effectively left intact and continues to be as before."[9] but consciousness, by taking possession of reality, as it were, "in terms of knowledge, installs in the subject a version or duplicate of reality by which the subject is enriched."[10]

So far we have been concerned with pointing out Romero's initial presentation of intentional consciousness as knowing the self as self, as perceiving objects and as characterized by the ability to name, to communicate, and to judge in each act of perception. For a further clarification of his own theory Romero introduces other views—not to criticize them for the sake of showing weaknesses in them but to make clearer his position as he indicates differences between these other views and his own. In stating that this clarification is his reason for discussing these other views, he mentions his lack of interest in polemics and says that he is sure that these other thinkers have very good reasons for their own theories.

Again we should make the comment that such an attitude toward theories which he does not share is indeed an indication of a great thinker who is interested in furthering the search for an understanding of the things which matter most rather than in trying to gain fame by belittling those whose theories differ from his. It is a position, by the way, which one wishes some candidates for office would adopt in an election year. Then the painting of false word pictures of opponents would cease and the contenders could work together in order to bring about a brighter tomorrow as each learns from the considered judgment of others. By thinking together they should be able to gain new insights hidden from the solitary thought of each. Thus, in the political sphere, the adoption of Romero's attitude would vitalize political life—to say nothing of what this attitude might do in other spheres.

But, specifically, what other views does Romero discuss? He has a few words to say about the will-for-power urge and notes that such lust is also present in animals. He says, for example, that Katz has reported observations made on hens. These show that, if two hens are in a coop together, one hen is going to dominate the other hen. On this observation Romero comments: "The partisans of a society rigidly stratified according to power may be surprised that their ideal is already realized in any chicken yard."[11] So much for Romero's way of putting gently in their place those who lust for power. However, to keep the record straight, Romero says that "the blind exercise of power is nothing but a primitive form of the assertion of individuality."[12] Yet more important is it to realize that, even if it is true that there is in man this desire to dominate, "something else completely alien to animal societies exists in man and that is the agelong fight against domination, beginning in the first ethical postulates and continuing in legislation, customs, and in the growing consciousness of equal rights for all."[13] Thus the spiritual attitude comes to the fore and blocks man's domination of his fellows. Consequently it is made quite evident that "history . . . is the history of liberty," as Hegel also saw.

Another view with which Romero is not in agreement is

that which regards the unique characteristic of man as spirit. If by spirit is meant that which exhibits a completely disinterested attitude and transcends narrow concerns, then one can not say that man is differentiated from other beings by spirit for this view fails to take into account man's intentionality, which initially characterizes him as distinct from other beings.

Again, some regard man as having no fixed nature—no uniqueness, distinguishing him from other living beings but as a mere happening and, as such, these theorizers think of man as his history. Romero regards this view as due partly to a reaction against an earlier position which envisions man as progressing steadily toward an established goal—or, as the poet has put it, man advances toward "one divine, far-off event to which the whole creation moves." The theory that man is simply an indefinable happening is due also, Romero thinks, to the current pessimism in some quarters concerning man. We might add that this pessimism finds expression in a form of phenomenological existentialism, unless it can be said that, since the claim is made that man is nothing then he must already have a fixed nature—if to be nothing can be thought of as a distinguishing characteristic. However that would imply that nothing is something. Hence essense is suggested and essence is precluded. Here we have an interesting paradox—one that reminds us of Alice's encounter with one of the queens in WONDERLAND. It will be recalled that one day Alice stood looking down the garden walk when the queen observed her doing this and asked at what she was gazing, Alice's reply was: "At nothing"; whereat the queen remarked: "What good eyes to see nothing and at that distance." But enough of this digression on phenomenological existentialism with its logically difficult concept of nothingness.

Now to return to Romero's own position on man's historicity, Romero points out that intentionality in man introduces norms which signify that man's existence is not mere arbitrariness, not a simple historical flux. Furthermore there is latent in intentionality spirit and spirit gives direction to man's activities. In other words, man's life exhibits purposiveness. Thus man is not like a leaf on a lake moved about only as the wind ruffles the surface of the lake—though Bergson thought that man often behaved in that fashion. For these reasons Romero does not share the view that man lives without purpose.

Moreover, Romero is not satisfied with the contention that the practical manipulation of things is the principal cause of man's gaining the ability to conceive of an objective world. Romero holds that, over against objects there must be a subject, characterized by intentionality, and thus knowing itself as subject in the presence of objects. One reason why such a view seems obvious to him is that the animal is confronted with the same objects and yet has not acquired the same subject-object understanding which man has been able to achieve. Hence man must already have had the capacity to understand that he is a subject in the presence of a world of objects in order for such understanding to develop in him when it appears not to have developed in the animal, even though the animal too engages in the practical manipulation of things in building a dam, or storing nuts for the winter, or otherwise manipulating things to preserve his life. Of course Romero is fully aware that the actual handling and working with objects is an important aid in comprehending them. Even so "it is not the hands that know, but the mind."[14]

Still another view discussed by Romero in order to clarify his own position is the theory held by some recent psychologists that the emotions and the will have a more important rôle than the intellect in the development of the human being. Romero maintains of course that the emotional and the impulsive aspects of the *psyche* are important. However, in so far as they are more than the states which they may have been in a pre-intentional stage, they are raised to the intentional level by the intellect. This is shown very clearly in the case of the will, which needs the designs of the intellect to operate effectively. The emotions also need the illumination which only the intellect can give. For example, where justice is at stake emotion alone can not determine the course which should be taken.[15]

In the light of Romero's discussion of these aspects of

other theories, it is obvious that intentionality is an activity which is different from the activity of the animal as he lives his everyday life. Human intentionality is an activity which "creates its own ends."[16] By means of intentionality as well as by means of spirit man creates his culture. Here Romero defines culture as an "illimitable series of acts and products in which man externalizes and gives expression to his innermost being, gives shape to it, supplying it with materials gathered from all sides and elaborates a world which is his own. Cultural objectifications, external expressions of his soul . . . serve him and at the same time sustain and support him."[17] While spirit creates the higher expressions of culture—such as religion and art—intentionality operates by introducing into the world "a powerful, restless energy which increases, modifies, reorganizes, and humanizes the world."[18] It is obvious, then, that the problem of culture needs to be considered at length and this will be done in a later chapter.

Romero's next concern is to investigate the human community in order to see whether it complements or corroborates his theory of man, as presented so far. His plan is not to do a sociological study and he will not yet be concerned with man's spiritual aspect. Even so he finds that the animal community differs from the human community. One fundamental fact is that the human community is made up of beings characterized by intentionality: beings who know themselves as subjects in the presence of an objective world—a knowledge which Romero thinks that even the higher animals possess only slightly, if at all. As for the fact that the human community is a group of beings who know themselves as subjects, this does not mean that the human being is at first fully conscious of himself as subject. One must be able to convert himself into an object in order to comprehend himself—a difficult procedure, as Auguste Comte once stated. That man originally lacks full self-consciousness is shown—Romero says—in primitive tribes as follows: when one of the members of the tribe commits a crime, the whole tribe is held responsible for the crime. The difficulty of attaining self-knowledge is highlighted during the adolescent period of the human being's life. This period is the time when one begins seriously to try to attain an understanding of himself. The result is that the adolescent period is a time of crisis. Of course in discussing the difficulty of attaining full comprehension of the self, Romero is not thinking of the egoism which is a kind of "practical self-affirmation." So much for a reminder that the human community is a community composed of beings who know the world as objective to them and who eventually attain at least some knowledge of themselves.

Another way in which the human community differs from the animal community is that the human community has the advantage of being made up of talkers. Romero points out that, through man's use of language, he can exchange ideas with others and thereby promote the development of thought. Furthermore, language is a way of preserving the funded knowledge of an age so that the knowledge can be passed on to the future generations—if not as knowledge at least as tradition.[19]

Romero cites the difference between tradition and traditionalism as he sees that difference. For him, tradition is enriching but traditionalism attempts to make "eternally present" a given practice or a given point of view. In primitive tribes and among animals traditionalism obtains. Tradition, on the other hand, furnishes a basis from which man can advance to new conquests.

Now a human community may become a human society. By *human society* Romero means "a group with norms and ends most clearly established."[20] Such a group may break up into smaller groups—each with its own norms and ends clearly defined. Each of these smaller groups develops consciousness of its own character as it observes the characteristics of other groups—characteristics which are different from those of the group observing. Thus there were Greeks and barbarians, Jews and gentiles.

What we have been saying on the basis of Romero's preliminary discussion of his theory concerning the human community is this: the human community or the human society is made up of individuals who can speak very precisely with each other, who have a tradition which enriches the current life, and who can develop norms and ends through thinking together. Hence this human society is not merely a perfected animal community but different from the latter.

Furthermore, the intentional consciousness which is a component of the beings making up the human community is initially responsible for the culture by which man surrounds himself; for by *culture* Romero means the results of man's objectivating activity. The functioning of the intentional component of man in producing culture comes about in this way. Man's ability to perceive the world of objects as such is linked with the tendency to create. In other words, "that which bestows on man objective comprehension of what is alien to him grants him the gift of creating and both functions are unified and inseparable."[21] Evidence of this tendency to express what has been perceived is shown "in the picture writings of the primitive, in the drawings of the child, and perhaps likewise in certain imitative postures."[22] That is, what one perceives "lodges" in him and demands to be given expression in outward form. There is also imaginative creation. Here the song, for example, seems to "sing in one's soul," or the doctrine appears to arouse the scientist to publish it so that its light may clarify the facts to which it refers.[23] Romero observes that of the many imaginings which are the lot of man only a few appeal to him as sound enough to receive creative expression. They appeal, for example, by their beauty, or by the splendor of "unpublished truth," or by the benefit which they seem capable of bringing. Sometimes the musician, or the scientist, or the inventor is not fully conscious of what impels him to create. Moreover, his song, or his new insight, or his utensil—designed to make everyday life easier—must find acceptance in the community if the creation is to become a part of the objective culture of the community. In this connection, it will be recalled that Browning counted on the eventual acceptance of his RING AND THE BOOK thus: "So, British Public, who may like me yet." Not only may the creator of an object of culture feel moved to express an inner imagining—a song or what not—but he may also feel that this is something which should be done; that the community needs the message which the song conveys.

What we have attempted so far in this chapter is to mention main points in Romero's theory of natural man. These points need more elaboration in order to make clear to the reader the basis on which they rest. For that elaboration, one should go directly to Romero's own writings, especially to his TEORIA DEL HOMBRE. After having done this, whether one agrees with Romero or not, he must appreciate Romero's carefully reasoned probing into the very difficult problem concerning man's basic nature. As we shall see in a later chapter,* there are psychologists who seem satisfied that it may be a thousand years before we have reliable knowledge about man's fundamental nature. But, as all must be fully aware, we are faced now with the need for as much light on that problem as we can get in order to understand as much as possible about ourselves and others.[24]

So far, then, we have noted that Romero concludes that minimal man has intentionality and this involves both a recognition of the self as subject and objectivating judgment. Due to this type of judgment, man has been able to recognize common characteristics in objects and by this means has progressed to universal concepts. This ability has made possible the development of intelligence and language. Furthermore, man, in association with other human beings, has been able to evolve human societies with clearly defined norms and purposes. These norms and purposes give direction to the life of a given society. Again, the activity of man, or of human beings working together, has brought into existence culture—man-made and in its turn acting on man to make him other than he would have been in a different environment.

However man who lacks spirit is not man "in the most complete sense of the word," Romero asserts.[25] He does say that spirit is latent in intentionality although spirit is not apparent in natural man, who lives as if he were the focal point of the world. That world, from his point of view, is seen in terms of his experiences—much as was the case of

---

* *Cf.* Chapter VII.

Heraclitus's frog as the frog sat on a log in a lake. Natural man's egocentricity is apparent in inferior peoples and also in some men belonging to superior groups. Yet the egocentricity of these peoples is not egoism in the derogatory sense of the term for they do have altruistic tendencies and such a man may even sacrifice for another who is like him.[26]

In general, nevertheless, the intentional act has in view the end which natural man has set for himself. On the other hand, the spiritual act is a transcendent act. A provisional definition of the spiritual act is this: "the spiritual act is that intentional act in which the subject applies itself to the object."[27] In other words, the private interests of the subject do not enter into the picture. In the spiritual act "a particle of divinity" is installed.[28] The mere intentional act and spiritual intentionality are distinguished, then, because in the latter case there is not the return to the ego. The purely intentional act does not complete its objective direction but there is a subjective regressus. It may be that this return is to "us" rather than to "me." That is, the return may be to "us the living, us as human beings, us Americans, those of our class, those of our family, us who are doctors, us who are sportsmen, us who are taxpayers, or us who smoke pipes."[29] The point is that there is not the absolute projection toward *the other* as is the case in the spiritual act, even though the intentional act may have a more extensive terminus than just the ego, yet lacks the absolute objectivity of the spiritual act. Furthermore, the subject who initiates the spiritual act is himself enlarged because he "has dispossessed himself of his equipment of individual interests and has converted what is alien into his interests."[30] The subject has thus gained liberty —freedom from private concerns. Romero thinks that, however different mere intentionality is from spirit, intentionality seems to be the basis for spirit. He reasons in this way: as one comes, through intentional activity, into contact with objects, he may eventually forget to look on himself as the center of reference and "finishes by recognizing the reality of each object in and for itself and perhaps comes to feel more or less vaguely that to refer these objects to himself in practice partially denies them and ignores the meaning of being in and for itself."[31]

By now it must be apparent that the whole question of the relation between natural man and man in whom spirit is developed calls for a chapter by itself. As we are about to enter on that discussion, we are reminded of what Socrates once said of beauty: "It is a subject for more than mortal discourse." The same might be said of the theme which we are about to explore under the guidance of Romero. Yet before doing that and hence before leaving this phase of the problem of the nature of natural man, we might well recall another examination of the subject, especially as Romero welcomes consideration of other views—holding that other thinkers have good reasons for their theories. In exploring the nature of primitive man Runes—as does Romero—notes the importance of speech which Runes finds to be "the great wonder of man's far-off antiquity."[32] He states that three hundred basic words which "are pretty much the same" are found among many peoples on the face of the earth. Moreover, he, like Romero, cites the importance of words in the development of knowledge. Runes's subsequent discussion of knowledge is very important for our troubled time.[33] His dramatic presentation of this subject should be read for its beauty as well as for its truth. Any attempt to give the gist of that presentation here could not possibly carry its poetic verity "alive to the heart." Hence we turn now to Romero's contrast between natural man and man who is more truly man because his spiritual component is developed.

REFERENCES

1. F. Romero, TEORIA DEL HOMBRE, Editorial Losada, S. A., Buenos Aires, 1952, p. 15.
2. *Ibid.*, p. 18.
3. *Ibid.*, p. 15.
4. *Ibid.*, p. 15; *cf.* also pp. 23 and 38.
5. Cf. *ibid.*, pp. 21-22.
6. *Ibid.*, p. 13.

7. *Cf. ibid.*, p. 60.
8. *Ibid.*, p. 56.
9. *Ibid.*, p. 19.
10. *Ibid.*, pp. 19-20.
11. *Ibid.*, p. 37.
12. *Ibid.*, p. 37.
13. *Ibid.*, pp. 37-38.
14. *Ibid.*, p. 27.
15. *Cf. ibid.*, pp. 33-34.
16. *Ibid.*, p. 83.
17. *Ibid.*, pp. 84-85.
18. *Ibid.*, p. 85.
19. *Cf. ibid.*, pp. 105-106.
20. *Ibid.*, p. 110.
21. *Ibid.*, p. 135.
22. *Ibid.*, p. 135.
23. *Cf. ibid.*, p. 136.
24. *Cf.* ACTAS DEL PRIMER CONGRESO ARGENTINO DE PSICOLOGIA, Vol. I, Ministerio de Educación de Nación—Universided Nacional de Tucumán, Tucumán, 1955, pp. 187 ff.
25. TEORIA DEL HOMBRE, p. 145.
26. *Cf. ibid.*, pp. 147 and 151.
27. *Ibid.*, p. 158.
28. *Ibid.*, p. 162.
29. *Ibid.*, p. 167.
30. *Ibid.*, p. 167.
31. *Ibid.*, pp. 168-169.
32. Dagobert Runes, ON THE NATURE OF MAN, Philosophical Library, New York, 1956. p. 28.
33. *Cf. ibid.*, pp. 71 ff.

Chapter IV

ON THE DUAL NATURE OF MAN

As has been indicated in the preceding chapter, Romero maintains that man who is most truly man is both natural man and man in whom spirit is developed. Romero points out that philosophical and religious thinkers through the ages have commented on the dual nature of man. That duality has been thought of in terms of body and soul and, more recently in some quarters, in terms of life and spirit. However, Romero thinks that man is best understood if he is thought of in terms of intentionality and spirituality because man in whom only intentionality appears present is much more than animal and hence to think of him partially in terms of body or even of life fails to take into account his difference from the animal.[1] In the preceding chapter we have been concerned with Romero's theory of natural or minimal man, whose principal component is intentionality and we have presented very briefly suggestions of Romero about spirit. Now we must give a more detailed account of Romero's theory of spirit.

Before noting the characteristics he gives of spirit, we should explain the significance of two terms often used by him in discussing the nature of man because he gives his own connotation of these terms. One is *individual* and the other is *person*. *Individual* is a psycho-physical being in whom intentionality is the organizing principle whereas *person* is a human being in whom spirit is the organizing principle.

The characteristics of the organizing principle of *person* —i.e., the characteristics of spirit—can best be seen if they are presented against a back drop on which very specifically and very succinctly is portrayed a word portrait of *individual*. He is self-centered. His immediate interests are dictated by his psycho-physical nature and are his guides to and the masters of his way of life. Thus he views other things and other human beings as they function in relation to him; as they benefit him or fail to do so.* Hence *reality* appears as relative to him who is a being not only of natural appetites and vital necessities but a being under the domination of contingent and evanescent interests. As a being thus swayed he is unstable and lacks freedom. Furthermore, he is in perennial conflict with other human beings who are determined by similar influences. Hobbes discussed this conflict in his description of what he designated as the state of nature. This *bellum omnium contra omnes* could be checked by an absolute monarch. However, Hobbes saw man only as *individual* and the absolute ruler has too often introduced absolute violence in order to maintain his position. Even today Hobbes' theory of human nature persists in some quarters. It is regarded as the realistic appraisal of man because it seems to be supported by some of the investigations of the nineteenth century. This false realism explains all from the level of *individual* and regards "person as a fiction."²

But *person* is not a fiction even though spirit—its organiz-

---

* We are not forgetting Romero's thought that minimal man does exhibit some altruism at times because he does, on occasion, sacrifice for his family or his associates or even for a larger group. But such an individual is obviously one in whom spirit is developing. Romero makes clear his view that, even in natural man, spirit appears present in germ. He, furthermore, notes the complexity of the problem of the nature of man and the necessity of considering that problem in connection with ideas on the reality which circumscribes him. *Cf.*, for example, TEORIA DEL HOMBRE, pp. 205-206. In a sense, what we are bringing together in this paragraph are statements which show *individual* as a statue rather than as a living being. However that would be the fate of any attempt to present in a nut shell Romero's conception of *individual*. His complete account of *individual* or natural man does full justice to the live human being.

ing principle—is a late comer on the scene. *Person* is a spiritual being. In order to make clear what Romero means by *person*, we shall bring together various of his statements on the subject—even though the sketchy result would probably be criticized by Socrates, were he living today, as a polished statue. However we hope to convey enough of Romero's thought on the subject so as not to do that thought injustice since we shall expect the reader to understand the problem involved in so brief a presentation of Romero's theory of person.

As a spiritual being, *person* is activity. But *person* is not only the whole of its acts and attitudes but it is the center from which these acts and these attitudes proceed. Its concern is not for useful knowledge in order to give it power but for insight into *what is*, regardless of any practical value to himself. *Person* would penetrate to the being or essence of each entity—including the innermost nature of *individual*—without thought of narrow benefit from this seeking to understand. But the outcome of this enterprise is that *person* is enriched thereby and yet leaves intact the objects among which its thought moves. *Person* has respect for *what is* unless *what is* does not measure up to what it should be. In such a case *person* attempts to raise *what is* to the standard it should attain, if there is any chance of promoting improvement. *Individual*, too, pretends such attempts and thus excuses its manipulation of objects, yet reduces them to furthering its own ends or destroys them; whereas, toward that which is but has not achieved what it was born to be, the attitude of *person* is helpful and not meddling. Toward the rest of reality *person's* attitude is cognitive, or ethical, or aesthetic, or religious—depending on that reality toward which *person* assumes an attitude. Furthermore *person* seeks the timeless values. Since *person* projects himself toward such values and strives for insight into reality, he attains a stability impossible for *individual*, concerned mainly with the contingent. In view of the fact that such attitudes and such striving are typical of *person*, it is obvious that those who are persons are not in a state of war as are individuals who produce and seek to procure utilitarian objects and are thus brought into conflict with each other on this lower level. And still further, Romero refers with approval to Ortega's theory of the programmatic character of *person*. Indeed they would probably agree with Browning that " 'tis not what man Does which exalts him but what man Would do!" That is, such is the case if what man proposes to do is not limited by selfish purposes—as is the case with schemes of *individual* —but is a suitable program for *person*. A suitable program is not one that is instigated by the counsel: "Live for today" or by the suggestion: "Take the line of least resistance." A suitable program is one which is seen "from the point of view of the stars." Such a program can be envisioned by *person* and instigated by him since it requires the objectivity and freedom of spirit, which is the organizing principle of *person*.[3]

In Alejandro Korn, Romero found one who was a real person. He had—Romero tells us—an "austere will for truth" and an extraordinary capacity for going to the source of things. He sought facts, but for him the universal shone through the fact. Early he had gained insight into the wider reality, into "the fundamental securities." This insight gave him a deep and genial optimism, which was not shaken by the dark side of life which had been revealed to him in his experience with men in politics, in hospitals, and in mental institutions. The hope which he could offer another in difficulty was therefore not shallow but firmly founded. He influenced others without interfering with their lives. His friendliness was of the elevated kind which did not descend to "trivial familiarity." Korn achieved an equanimity which was unshaken by good or ill fortune. He believed that man had in him "the capacity to go forward and upward"; that man could become progressively free and that freedom is creative.[4]

From this glimpse—so to speak—of a real person, we turn to consider explicitly the characteristics of spirit, which are revealed in a real person whereas intentionality is the predominant component of *individual*. Yet it must not be forgotten that, according to Romero, both intentionality and spirit are present in varying degrees in the normal human being. As has already been indicated in discussing *person*, spirit is marked by absolute objectivity; spirit is "occupied with the object entirely." Hence, in the realm of cognition, spirit has a "disinterested interest" in the object and seeks to know it completely; whereas, in the intentional act which aims at cognition, the knowledge desired is that which will have practical value for the subject. Therefore, in this latter case, knowledge of the object is only partial knowledge. In the ethical act, spirit is interested in promoting "an order which is justified and valuable" and not in furthering private schemes for the subject.[5]

A second fundamental characteristic of spirit is universality. Spirit is not content with being immersed in the particulars of the natural realm but seeks a reality beyond these particulars. It seeks "the good, the lovely, and the true, and types whose earthly copies are the foolish, broken things we knew"—to put this search in the words of Rupert Brooke. In this connection one is reminded of a criticism Enrique Molina once made of pragmatism. He feels that pragmatism stays too close to the more mundane interests and thus seeks the type of knowledge which will enable man to dominate rather than to understand his world.[6] In other words, Molina's opinion is that the pragmatist takes the intentional rather than the spiritual attitude toward the world and thus does not desire to understand it but merely to gain the competence to appropriate these parts of it which will serve a useful purpose.*

A third fundamental characteristic of spirit is freedom. It should be observed that, since spirit is free, it is characterized naturally by objectivity and by universality. That is, these traits go hand in hand with freedom. The special freedom which spirit enjoys is freedom from "the propensities and attitudes of the natural man."[7] Obviously this freedom has to be attained by effort. Such freedom Korn also had in mind. And this freedom would be a real kind of freedom for Tagore, who once wrote that freedom should not be a gift

---

* The aim here is not to criticize pragmatism from our viewpoint but simply to give an illustration of the significance of the intentional rather than the spiritual attitude.

because only the freedom which is won is the freedom which is understood. Since Korn held that freedom of the spirit is freedom from egocentricity, he felt it to be "the destiny of person to guard always the totality within him as a conjunction of the real and the ideal" taking care, with regard to the real, to preserve what should be ours and to subdue in us what should be subdued and, with regard to the ideal, seeing to it that what should be brought about is attained.[8]

Moreover, there is evident—especially in the cognitive and in the ethical attitudes of spirit—unity of spirit for spirit "obeys the demands of reason, the strict rules of logic . . . and recognizes the fundamental, ethical postulates." This is in contrast to the diversity in the man who is governed by his subjective interests which are often in conflict. Romero says that this unity of spirit has been recognized since antiquity. For example, the mission of Socrates was to show the identity of concepts and norms which reason attains. Romero regards *reason* as Socrates thought of it to be another name for spirit as Romero uses that term.[9]

As has been implied in discussing freedom as an achievement of spirit, it has a history. In the foregoing chapter we noted that Romero regards intentionality as the basis of spirit and the following is a reason—as we there stated. In intentional activity one may become interested in an object for itself. Where this occurs he ceases to think of its advantage to him or of its effect on him. When this interest in the object for its own sake takes place, man has adopted the spiritual rather than the intentional attitude toward that object. Romero thinks that the spiritual attitude blossoms in "established maturity when the mere intentional function has become fixed"; that is, when the intentional acts take place in their proper area and thus do not comprise the main activity of the human being. Romero goes on to say that only through historical conquest do spiritual acts become habitual. Furthermore, among those who are naturally genial, spiritual acts are more likely to flower. Also, in a community enjoying a long philosophical and scientific tradition, spiritual acts have more chance of being initiated. Still further, a community favored with aesthetic creations will facilitate the increase of spiritual acts.[10]

All these characteristics of spiritual acts make it obvious that there are certain secondary characteristics of the spiritual attitude such as respect for all, interest in all, and a feeling of responsibility for one's own acts which aim at bettering the lives of all. At times such acts achieve heroic and sacrificial dimensions. At times even, the being in whom spirit is fully developed feels responsibility for the stupidity and the evil in the world.[11]

But more important than all these characteristics is the essential characteristic of spirit, i.e., absolute transcendence. This, Romero thinks, should be treated separately and hence we shall do that in the next chapter. What remains now for us to do is to come to grips with the question of the relation between the intentional attitude and the spiritual attitude in the single human being and also with the problem of stimulating spiritual acts. Romero says that "spiritual acts are intentional acts of a special kind, characterized by total objective projection."[12] That is, in the spiritual act, there is no return to the self, no expectation of personal reward such as —we might suggest—favorable publicity or even just a few moments of occupying the limelight. The question of the relation between the intentional and the spiritual attitudes in a single human being can of course be answered only in generalities because each man is a special case. In general, a human being has more intentional moments than spiritual ones except for men of exceptional spiritual caliber. Yet because of the superiority of the spiritual moments, they amount to more in the final result. Again, Romero thinks that the intentionality of man makes for a certain kind of stability which keeps him in contact with *what is*, even though that intentionality may need domestication by the spiritual component.[13]

In adolescence there is quite often a clash between the intentional and the spiritual components of the youth. For example, he may have an idealized love for another at times and that affection may be of a more carnal sort at other times. Hence it is difficult to maintain always the spiritual attitude toward the loved one. It is a function of the teacher, Romero thinks, to help the youth to resolve the forces clashing within him so that he may achieve "a full and harmonious life under the inspiration of superior interests."[14] Romero feels that maturity brings some reconciliation of the two components of man's nature. With maturity each man has gained some competence in working out a pattern for his way of life and thus reduces the clashing of the two components of his nature. He may serve as an example to his neighbors of the way in which life should be lived and thus help them with their own problems. Great personalities do bring about changes in those who come into contact with them.* On the other hand, a community may help a member of that community to overcome hypocrisy or weakness by letting him know that these traits are recognized and by stimulating him to live on a higher plane, by helping him to take more often the spiritual attitude. Again, shock may bring about a change in the pattern of life the mature man follows. Conversion is an instance where such a change takes place. Still further, the culture of a locality has an effect on those who live in that city, or that province, or that state. Since this is the case, Romero says that culture must become more spiritual in order to promote a more spiritual way of life.[15]

Thus whether one man, through his insight into the meaning of human life, brings about the triumph of his spiritual component over his intentional component, or whether great personalities, or shock, or culture accomplish this triumph, human advance requires this victory. Romero's counsel, then, is like that of Socrates, i.e., that man "hold fast to the heavenly way"—which is the course prescribed by the spiritual component. To illustrate this point, we might think in terms of a rider and his horse rather than in terms of Plato's myth of the charioteer because, in this latter case, there is envisaged a tripartite division of man's inner nature. The rider should

---

* Romero would not accept completely James' thesis in his "Great Men and Their Environment" for Romero states that man owes infinitely more to culture than he contributes no matter how brilliant that contribution. (*Cf.* TEORIA DEL HOMBRE, p. 258)

be a doctor who is in a hurry to save the life of a patient. To win this race against death the rider and his horse must be as one and yet the horse must obey the guiding hand of his rider. The rider of course represents the spiritual element and the horse represents the intentional element of man's nature. A better illustration would be provided by certain points made by Ortega in his "How to Make and Break a Nation."[16] This is a better illustration from our contemporary point of view because no doctor whom we know today rides a horse to a sick bed. We shall present the thought of this essay in modified form because we shall introduce the terms *intentional component* and *spiritual component*. However, this introduction should not do injustice to the thought of the essay. For the most part the essay is concerned with accounting for the accomplishments of King Ferdinand and with explaining the subsequent weakening of his nation. Ferdinand overcame the particularism of Spain—the striving of his subjects to further each his own narrow ends, the striving of his intentional component. The king stirred the dormant spiritual component in each of his subjects by presenting to them "great and inspiring enterprises" and by promoting "high moral, religious, and judicial ideals." Thus, under his leadership, Spain became great. Subsequently sectionalism became a ruling factor—or we might say the people of Spain lost sight of these high goals and the intentional component became again the ruler of the destiny of each. Down through the years there has been sectionalism and, furthermore, Ortega wrote, each department has sought its own, narrow ends as if government existed for a given department. We might present this situation in terms of *individual* and *person*, in the sense in which they have been explained earlier. Then we would say that men in each department have been acting as individuals rather than as persons; their intentional components have been the guiding factors and their spiritual components have been in abeyance. Thus they have been seeking their private advantages rather than the welfare of all, as persons would do. It should be added here that it is never possible for a student of Kantian philosophy to suggest an illustration without recalling that Kant once called examples the gocarts of the imagination. However, in the present state of world affairs, it is very difficult not to apply to current problems what Romero has said concerning individual and person and their intentional and spiritual functions. In the light of Romero's lucid analysis, one sees more clearly and possibly less passionately a central problem of our contemporary crisis. However we have purposely adapted this illustration from Ortega because it is easier to *think* about past events than about what is transpiring in the cold war.

However it is now time to explore the nature of the transcendence, which Romero regards as the primary characteristic of spirit.[17] And it is well that we should do so for the subject takes us beyond the strife of individuals, who can not understand one of the difficulties with which persons are faced: persons must respect the rights of others; as persons they can not violate these rights. This is a difficulty only because persons must find other means than brute force to guard against the violence of individuals.

REFERENCES

1. *Cf.* TEORIA DEL HOMBRE, pp. 240-244.
2. *Cf.* FILOSOFIA DE LA PERSONA, pp. 10, 20, 24-26, 42-46 and also Romero and Eugenio Pucciarelli, LOGICA (Décima Edición), Espasa-calpe Argentina, S. A. Buenos Aires, 1947, p. 204.
3. *Cf.* FILOSOFIA DE LA PERSONA, pp. 8-12, 20, 24-25, 30-32, 40, 44-48, and also FILOSOFIA DE AYER Y DE HOY, pp. 241-242.
4. *Cf.* ALEJANDRO KORN, pp. 14-24.
5. *Cf.* TEORIA DEL HOMBRE, pp. 190-192.
6. *Cf.* Enrique Molina, DE LO ESPIRITUAL EN LA VIDA HUMANA, Editorial Nascimento, Santiago de Chile, pp. 19-20.
7. TEORIA DEL HOMBRE, p. 194.
8. *Cf.* ALEJANDRO KORN, p. 47.
9. TEORIA DEL HOMBRE, pp. 193-194.
10. *Cf. ibid.*, pp. 196-197.
11. *Cf. ibid.*, pp. 197-198.

12. *Cf. ibid.*, p. 250.
13. *Cf. ibid.*, pp. 250-251.
14. *Ibid.*, p. 253.
15. *Cf. ibid.*, pp. 253-258.
16. This is the first essay in Ortega's INVERTEBRATE SPAIN (tr. M. Adams) W. W. Norton & Company, Inc., 1937.
17. Juan Carlos Torchia Estrada regards the idea of transcendence as the central idea of Romero's metaphysical writings. *Cf.* Estrada's article "La Concepción Antropológica de Francisco Romero" in CIUDAD, secundo y tercer trimestre 1956, Buenos Aires, p. 22.

Chapter V

TRANSCENDENCE

As we have already noted in the preceding chapter, Romero regards absolute transcendence as the primary characteristic of spirit, which is the highest plane of reality. The other three planes—the physical, life, and intentional psyche—do exhibit a degree of transcendence, since each of the first three supports and fosters the plane which succeeds it. On the physical plane, transcendence is not very evident but it still takes place. Thus, for example, the elements hydrogen and oxygen transcend themselves to become water, for water is not just hydrogen plus oxygen but is something other than their sum. Water is the result of this transcendence through which, under definite conditions, hydrogen and oxygen "actualize certain properties in both."[1] But another aspect of the physical plane rather than the transcendence taking place there made that plane attractive to the rationalists, Romero thinks. The substantiality, so to speak, of the physical plane was the basis for the idea that a very rigorous pattern of reality could be outlined and this was the reason why the rationalists were satisfied with expounding the nature of reality in terms of the physical. On this basis they evolved a very fixed and—to them—a very certain picture of reality, unmindful of the poet's warning: "Oh what a dusty answer gets the soul when hot for certainties in this our life." Next, the plane of life shows the characteristic of transcendence more clearly. Thus, for example, there is a sense in which offspring transcend their progenitors.[2]

But it is on the plane of the intentional psyche that transcendence is more evident, for "intentionality consists precisely in transcending toward the object. The subject is the point of departure of innumerable, continuous, transcendent acts, and the horizon for such acts is practically unlimited."[3] However, these acts are not completely transcendent because the merely intentional individual performs his acts in order to further his personal affairs; whereas, on the plane of spirit, "the subject, we can say, is the point of departure of the act" but not the point of return, so to speak. That is, the purpose of the spiritual person is not to achieve his ends in order to further his private interests, as is the case with the merely intentional individual, who is not activated by spirit. "The spiritual subject is the focus of transcendences."[4] But we must be more specific about the difference between the acts of the merely intentional individual, concerned with advancing his selfish schemes, and those of *person*, whose acts are fostered by spirit. First, however, we should note in resumé that "the different planes, from the physical to the spiritual, show . . . an increase of transcendence and the steps by which the spiritual has been raised above the physical can be interpreted as a series of successive and each time more perfect ways of transcending invented by reality in order to realize its truth."[5]

Now for a more specific statement concerning the difference between the transcendent acts of the individual and those of the spiritual person, it should be noted that the former is the center of his universe. He begins by viewing objects, not in their own right, but from the point of view of their contribution to his convenience. He appropriates the object. "The individual devours or enslaves; he always destroys the object, be it either its law, its meaning, or its autonomy."[6] He lives in perpetual conflict, unmindful of the rights and aspirations of others. We have mentioned in the preceding chapter Romero's allusion to Hobbes' lurid analysis of a state made up of men who are merely intentional beings, in whom spirit is not developed. These individuals have their attention turned inward, each seeking his own good, or—better—his own supposed good, if not "at the whole world's cost" at least at the cost of that portion of the world which seems at cross purposes to his own grasping aims, to his own seeking for those things which make for "commodious living."

On the other hand, men activated by spirit are not antagonistic to each other. Romero gives us a reason and it is this: the spiritual act is performed without reference to the subject "except for the inevitable connection between the subject and his act."[7] There must be such a connection for "there must be a center that transcends," otherwise there would be no transcendence, simply evaporation. That is, there must be a transcending being and "not a relinquishing of being" in order that a transcendent act can be performed.[8] Furthermore, the subject is enriched by this act of transcendence. We might suggest that such a subject might use the words of Tennyson's Ulysses and say of himself: " 'I am a part of all that I have met' "; or it might be said that what this subject has known disinterestedly or enjoyed aesthetically or performed to promote value has entered into him, as it were, and has made of him a more catholic man than the individual who is isolated by his selfishness and greed. Romero puts the matter this way: "The subject has the potentiality of living a life of infinite or illimitable radius."[9] This way of phrasing the point is similar to Nettleship's suggestion that the complete person lacks an environment.[10] Romero calls attention to the fact that the acts of transcendence of person are referred to as disinterested or altruistic acts as contrasted with the interested or egoistic acts of the intentional individual.[11] Obviously persons motivated by spirit work for spiritual values.

The need so to work is emphasized in Romero's mind by the crisis through which we have been and still are living. In 1943 he stated that a philosophy of the crisis is necessary —"a philosophy which eludes interested and partial valuations and elevates itself to an exact comprehension of the prodigious event." In such meditation man must "possess himself by himself, illumine his own being and be each time more master of himself and of his natural and cultural environment." Such a task is dependent on person's "conceiving himself as a bearer of spirit," and hence he must see himself "as an entity in whom the call of the spirit, infirm in its origins, gains strength, develops, and progresses toward its distant triumph, creating in its course the sphere of culture which embodies and executes its purposes." Romero believes that the advance toward a spiritual order "does not make sense if it is not thought of as a community of free persons."[12] But a community of free persons will not be working toward the goals of "the people," for such activity is not genuine transcendence but is a new kind of egoism, "a collective egoism tinged with mystical obscurity and gilded with an impressive though false prestige."[13] Rather, the acts of transcendence of free persons are directed toward values.

Values, according to Romero, are not subjective—are not "determined by the evaluation of the subject."[14] "Value is the measure of transcendence and, for that reason, of the actual reality of being: in each instance—being or activity—it is the dignity which belongs to it because of the transcendence it incarnates: on the part of the subject evaluating, this dignity is apprehended by a special emotion."[15] In other words, the worth, the value of a certain type of philosophic work, for example, is the degree to which the author has been able to transcend the passing show and to give us insight into what matters most, into the ultimate meaning of human existence. Moreover, the result of such penetration on the part of the author arouses a special emotion in the reader. Thus value itself is objective and is the gauge of transcendence and value has an attractiveness which arouses emotion.

In his further discussion of value and its link with transcendence, Romero examines two of the types of value: the cognitive and the ethical. Of cognitive value, he says that "when an object is examined faithfully . . . without adding the individual reaction . . . the transcendent movement is fundamental" because to gain genuine knowledge there must be "a placing of ourselves, as it were, in something foreign to us."[16] That is, we have here the cognitive counterpart of the emphatic experience. We have here a description of what must take place in a "disinterested interest" in gaining knowledge. The search for knowledge is a transcending action and the knowledge so obtained will be of theoretic value only so far as it is a mirror, so to speak, which "keeps intact the image of something which is essentially foreign to it and outside of it."[17] Thus Romero emphasizes the point that spiritual acts to obtain knowledge aim at penetrating into the object, without regard for its usefulness to the person who thus acts. Hence the value of such acts lies "in the clear transcendence of the act" and not in the truth obtained, although, if the act is one of full transcendence, the knowledge gained will be the truth.

On the other hand, in intentional cognition, the subject is not interested in the object for itself but he wants what knowledge he can acquire about the object only for the practical benefit which it can bring to him. In other words, knowledge is sought by the intentional individual for power. Hence his act of cognitive transcendence is not an act of complete transcendence and there its value is limited.[18]

Transcendence is exhibited by the ethical as well as by the purely cognitive act. But there is this difference between the two types of act. In cognitive transcendence, "one applies oneself to the object, assenting to that which is, pronouncing on the basis of comprehension: 'this is so' "; whereas, in ethical transcendence, one works to make *this* so because the ethical act is ethical by virtue of its "adherence to a norm or to a supra-individual value."[19] That is, the ethical act "is regulated by transcendence itself."[20] Hence "absolute ethical value exists only in the absolutely transcendent act."[21] Such a theory of ethical value is not foreign to a generally accepted position on such value. Romero reminds us that the term *altruism* suggests transcendence, whereas *egoism* implies a turning inward or immanence. Of egoism he says that "there is no other sin in strict ethics than egoism . . . hence the curious impression of limitation and stupidity, of spiritual cloudiness which evil is accustomed to produce."[22] In contrast, "the moral act tends toward extra-individual ends and brings the subject outside himself, to the air and light, and stretches out somewhat like the extended and gracious gesture of the athlete who throws the discus."[23] Romero cites the Golden Rule and Kant's categorical imperatives as indicating that the ethical act is a transcendent act, for this rule and these imperatives indicate objectivity and universality, which are characteristics of transcendence. The imperative which Romero formulates is as follows: "So act that the direction of your act concurs with the essential direction of reality."[24]

In view of this imperative it is well to consider what is involved in duty toward other beings. Romero says that obligation extends to all entities that transcend, even if that transcendence is only partial. But, in a given case, the amount of obligation is determined by the degree of transcendence. However, in the case of the human being, one must take into account the fact that man is potentially spirit even when his acts reveal little of genuine transcendence. Hence, even if spirit is not apparent in a given human being, it is one's duty to treat him as a person in whom spirit is present because, by so doing, the dutiful person will help to develop spirit in the being who has spirit only potentially.[25] Romero's position is very important for there is too great a tendency today to view human beings from the biological standpoint, forgetting that what makes man truly man is spirit and that "spirit is pure transcendence."[26]

So far we have been concerned with what is central in Romero's discussion of the transcendent act and with the relation between value and transcendence—especially in the areas of cognitive and ethical values. We shall next refer very briefly to what Romero says concerning certain historical periods of transcendence. In other words, we shall now see transcendence "writ large" —to adapt a phrase from Plato. Romero regards the medieval period as an age of transcendence because of the importance given in that era to faith, tradition, authority, and divine right. He regards the modern period until Romanticism as an age of immanentism because man was then thought of as having within himself reason capable of directing his way of life and perhaps even of arriving at that certain truth which Descartes sought so eagerly. Furthermore, man by virtue of being man, had certain rights and a conscience competent to guide him in religious matters. Such were the convictions in the modern era until the advent of Romanticism, which fostered transcendence without fully realizing its import. This claim with regard to Romanticism can be made because certain concepts were nourished in this period—concepts which involve transcendence in some way. The most typical and the most important of these concepts are structure and evolution. *Structure* includes the notion that "the parts transcend themselves in entering into the whole" as well as the notion that the whole transcends its parts. As for *evolution*, it is obvious that this concept implies transcendence.[27]

Romero's historical survey, which has here been so briefly indicated, calls to mind what others have said when they have been considering characteristics of historical periods. It seems fitting to mention the following. In line with Romero's commendation of the middle ages as an era of transcendence, we find Hocking's reference to the importance of the detached and the attached attitudes in this period—the detachment from mundane concerns and the attachment to values beyond this world.[28] These attitudes imply transcendence. Then Romero's characterization of the modern period before Romanticism as a time when man's attitude was an immanentistic one reminds us of Whitehead's ascription of a subjective tinge to modern philosophy.[29]

Turning now to another aspect of Romero's discussion of transcendence, we recall here main points in Romero's paper written for the second Inter-American Congress of Philosophy. In that paper—it will be remembered—Romero pointed out that the great cultures are probably characterized by "the formula of spiritual transcendence which they have used as their foundation." But he points out a difference between transcendence in India and China and transcendence in the Occident. In India, man seeks to transcend himself, that is to escape from the "particularity" and "transitoriness" which are characteristics of him. He denies himself and seeks reintegration with "metaphysical or cosmic totality."* In China the fleeing from the self, so to speak, is thought of in two ways: by the Taoists as "compenetration with the cosmic

---

* This attitude toward life suggests the melancholy of the poet who yearned to become one with "the sullen hardihood" of the yew tree.

sense" and by others as reintegration with the family, the state, entire society. Briefly, then, in these Asiatic cultures man seeks to give significance to his life by transcending toward realities which are external to him, "diluting in these realities his own individuality." In the Occident, on the other hand, transcendence is not an act of denial of the self, of resignation. The man of the Occident transcends in each of his acts when the act is directed toward "triumphant reality." Hence for Western man actions, time, and history are important because it is in time that he achieves what is historically significant.[30]

Still further, it is in the direction of transcendence that philosophy will be oriented in the future, Romero believes. One reason which he gives for this assumption is that one of the paths of transcendence is time and only now, he thinks, is there genuine interest in temporalism. Of this present interest in time Romero says: "After a delay of many centuries temporalism comes forward to claim for itself one of the principal rôles in the metaphysical drama." This indifference to time has been due largely to interest in essences rather than in "living, throbbing existences." Thus St. Augustine reasoned on time's essence. He claimed no extension for time because he viewed it as an ideal line between the past, which has ceased to exist, and the future, which has not arrived. "Thus real time appears before reason deprived of being and body." Hence St. Augustine pronounced time to be irrational. Later, Nicolas of Cusa laid the basis for the modern idealist conception of mathematical time, according to Cassirer, and Romero accepts his pronouncement. Kant "strengthened this concept rebuilding it on new and solid—though not irreproachable—cognitive foundations." In general post-Kantian idealism accepted this view. However Hegel did presage the later appreciation of temporalism. Yet, as a concession to rationalism, his *becoming* was an atemporalistic becoming—it was a dialectical becoming. Dilthey was one of the first to really appreciate time. But, "though rich in intuitions," he was frequently contradictory. Simmel views transcendence as the main point in a metaphysics of life and he senses life—as subjectively lived—as temporal reality. Simmel's *transcendence* is very much like Bergson's *duration*. Bergson noted that philosophers had arranged time and space in the same line and hence had not appreciated time. He thought of time or duration as "heterogeneous, qualitative, creative." He thought that homogeneous space and homogeneous time were "neither the property of things, nor the essential condition of our faculty of knowing them." He thought of them as "simply schemes of our action upon matter." Only lived time is real time, he thought. In spite of Bergson's appreciation of lived time, Romero thinks that he did not sufficiently appreciate transcendence but reduced it to duration, whereas Romero thinks of duration or time as only one path of transcendence. Such are merely some of Romero's remarks on past and recent views concerning time. Even all his remarks he regards as too sketchy, and his appraisal of his remarks indicates how little a resumé—such as that given here—can say.[31]

Important as Romero believes temporalism to be as one of the paths of transcendence, he thinks that there must be harmonious working of the temporal and the ideal orders for each to gain its fulness. He says: "Perhaps the cosmic drama consists in the very laborious adjustment . . . of the two orders: the temporal and the atemporal."[32]

Romero's prognosis that philosophy will be oriented in the direction of the transcendent raises the hope that philosophy will become again a way of life rather than, as in some quarters, a matter of words. If this hope is realized, philosophy will supply the need for the high view and the wide view, and the culture created as a result of this elevated outlook will surround man with that which is befitting one in whom spirit is developed. We turn now to consider, in the next chapter, basic points in Romero's ontology of culture.

REFERENCES

1. PAPELES PARA UNA FILOSOFIA, Editorial Losada, S. A., Buenos Aires, 1945, p. 26.
2. *Cf.* TEORIA DEL HOMBRE, pp. 207-208.
3. *Ibid.,* p. 208.
4. *Ibid.,* p. 209.
5. *Ibid.,* p. 213.

6. FILOSOFIA DE LA PERSONA, p. 43. *Cf.* also pp. 41-49.
7. TEORIA DEL HOMBRE, p. 200.
8. *Cf. ibid.*, p. 201.
9. PAPELES PARA UNA FILOSOFIA, p. 36.
10. *Cf.* PHILOSOPHICAL LECTURES AND REMAINS OF RICHARD LEWIS NETTLESHIP (Macmillan & Co., London, 1901, p. 34.
11. TEORIA DEL HOMBRE, p. 201.
12. FILOSOFOS Y PROBLEMAS, Editorial Losada, S. A., Buenos Aires, 1947, pp. 156-157.
13. PAPELES PARA UNA FILOSOFIA, p. 28.
14. TEORIA DEL HOMBRE, p. 213.
15. *Ibid.*, pp. 213-214.
16. PAPELES PARA UNA FILOSOFIA, p. 35.
17. *Ibid.*, p. 36.
18. *Cf.* TEORIA DEL HOMBRE, p. 222.
19. PAPELES PARA UNA FILOSOFIA, p. 42.
20. *Ibid.*, p. 43.
21. TEORIA DEL HOMBRE, p. 231.
22. PAPELES PARA UNA FILOSOFIA, pp. 41-42.
23. *Ibid.*, p. 42.
24. TEORIA DEL HOMBRE, p. 235.
25. *Cf. ibid.*, pp. 231-232.
26. *Ibid.*, p. 233.
27. *Cf.* PAPELES PARA UNA FILOSOFIA, pp. 9-12, 21-27.
28. *Cf.* THOUGHTS ON DEATH AND LIFE, Harper and Brothers, New York, 1937, pp. 141-142.
29. *Cf.* SCIENCE AND THE MODERN WORLD, New American Library of World Literature, Inc., New York, 1952, p. 140.
30. *Cf.* PAPERS AND ABSTRACTS OF THE SECOND INTER-AMERICAN CONGRESS OF PHILOSOPHY, American Philosophical Association, 1947, pp. 80-88.
31. *Cf.* FILOSOFIA CONTEMPORANEA, pp. 27-30 and 42-48.
32. *Ibid.*, p. 54.

CHAPTER VI

TOWARD AN ONTOLOGY OF CULTURE

In the foregoing chapter, one point brought out was that Western man, in transcending toward "triumphant reality," acts. One result of such action is creation of culture. Matthew Arnold once defined culture as "the disinterested endeavor after man's perfection."[1] Culture pursues this perfection "by means of getting to know, on all matters which most concern us, the best which has been thought and said in the world, and through this knowledge, turning a stream of fresh and free thought upon our stock notions and habits."[2] In other words, culture provides us with knowledge of the best thought and thus enables us to revivify our ideas and our habits. In commenting on this view of culture, Thomas Huxley states that Arnold thinks that literature alone is adequate for the task of supplying such knowledge. Naturally Huxley points out the necessity for acquaintance with "purely scientific disciplines" also and his stand is well taken. He holds rightly that humanists do not possess "the monopoly of culture."[3] Romero thinks of culture in an even more inclusive sense—as we saw in Chapter III. There we noted that Romero states that culture may be created by intentionality as well as by spirit—though spirit creates the high types of culture. Romero of course gives various definitions of culture. The one which quite briefly indicates the wide area covered by *culture* as Romero understands it is the following: culture is "constituted by the products of man's activity."[4] The domain of culture includes for him, then, "works of art, science, philosophy, religion, myth, language, morals as practiced, the state of all kinds of political and social organizations, technical products of all kinds." In short, Romero includes in culture all that "man has created and modified, and even the creative activity itself."[5]

Furthermore it should be noted that some cultural objects are the result of collective activity—either conscious or unconscious—whereas other products are the consequence of the activity of individuals. Examples of the former products are, of course, science, language, the state, customs. In the case of products created by individuals the following should be noted. It seems—Romero says—"as if the author sometimes was only the interpreter . . . of a social sentiment."[6] Thus Descartes sought to work out his own philosophy "but few systems have surpassed Cartesianism in being the faithful expression of a historical occasion."

However, whether objects of culture have been created by means of collective action or by individuals, Romero maintains that we are in need of a theory of culture which views culture as "a connected or unitary subject."[7] Such is the way that the Greeks of the ancient world viewed matter. That is, they conceived of the diversified objects of nature as primarily of one stuff, such as water, or air, or fire. This way of picturing external nature resulted in their not seeing the trees for the forest. In other words, they "neglected a careful and rigorous analysis and classification of . . . natural phenomena."[8] On the other hand, the objects of culture have been investigated separately. Only lately has there been the realization that the infinite variety of cultural objects are "psycho-physical objectifications—in spite of, or even beyond their diversity," and thus they should be viewed in a more integrated way. Spencer was the first, Romero thinks to adopt this standpoint but he presented only a brief and inadequate sketch of culture.

What should an adequate theory of culture include? According to Romero, a total theory of culture rests on three pillars: the ontological, the epistemological, and the axiological. It is with the first—the ontological—that we are concerned here together with certain comments on his standpoint.

Before embarking on an exploration of the *being* of culture, it seems well to Romero initially to illustrate the complexity of the problem by noting one of the diverse criteria which has been used in classifying cultural objects and processes.[9] The criterion which he chooses is that of value. But one can see quickly that such a classification is not easy to make. For example, a chair may be a practical piece of furniture and an object of high aesthetic worth.[10] Is the chair to be classified on the basis of its usefulness or is it to be classified on the basis of its beauty? In the case of language, the problem of classifying in accordance with value is a much more complicated one, for language fulfills various purposes: its aim may be expressive, or communicative, or dictatorial, or exorcistical—to name a few possibilities. These two examples which Romero chooses illustrate very clearly the difficulty of using the category of value as a means of classifying cultural objects and processes.

Having been forewarned by these illustrations of the perplexities which we can expect in arriving at an ontology of culture, we turn to a short survey of Romero's discussion of the subject. We shall begin with noting two types of investigation necessary in exploring the *being* of cultural objects. Then we shall consider his view of the "identical being" of objective culture. Finally we shall observe points suggested by his view of this "identical being of human culture which is common for all its diverse divisions."

First, then, concerning the two types of investigation necessary in exploring the being of cultural objects. It is a task for a general theory of culture to study the being of various kinds of cultural objects. Such investigation would break down into the exploration of the being of religious dogma, of works of art, of customs, and of many other kinds of cultural objects and processes. But there is also a further task for a general theory of culture—a task of greater dimensions—and that is none other than the task of exploring the common denominator of culture.[11] It is especially to this problem that Romero directs his attention.

the gocarts of the imagination. However, in the present state of world affairs, it is very difficult not to apply to current problems what Romero has said concerning individual and person and their intentional and spiritual functions. In the light of Romero's lucid analysis, one sees more clearly and possibly less passionately a central problem of our contemporary crisis. However we have purposely adapted this illustration from Ortega because it is easier to *think* about past events than about what is transpiring in the cold war.

However it is now time to explore the nature of the transcendence, which Romero regards as the primary characteristic of spirit.[17] And it is well that we should do so for the subject takes us beyond the strife of individuals, who can not understand one of the difficulties with which persons are faced: persons must respect the rights of others; as persons they can not violate these rights. This is a difficulty only because persons must find other means than brute force to guard against the violence of individuals.

REFERENCES

1. *Cf.* TEORIA DEL HOMBRE, pp. 240-244.
2. *Cf.* FILOSOFIA DE LA PERSONA, pp. 10, 20, 24-26, 42-46 and also Romero and Eugenio Pucciarelli, LOGICA (Décima Edición), Espasa-calpe Argentina, S. A. Buenos Aires, 1947, p. 204.
3. *Cf.* FILOSOFIA DE LA PERSONA, pp. 8-12, 20, 24-25, 30-32, 40, 44-48, and also FILOSOFIA DE AYER Y DE HOY, pp. 241-242.
4. *Cf.* ALEJANDRO KORN, pp. 14-24.
5. *Cf.* TEORIA DEL HOMBRE, pp. 190-192.
6. *Cf.* Enrique Molina, DE LO ESPIRITUAL EN LA VIDA HUMANA, Editorial Nascimento, Santiago de Chile, pp. 19-20.
7. TEORIA DEL HOMBRE, p. 194.
8. *Cf.* ALEJANDRO KORN, p. 47.
9. TEORIA DEL HOMBRE, pp. 193-194.
10. *Cf. ibid.*, pp. 196-197.
11. *Cf. ibid.*, pp. 197-198.

be a doctor who is in a hurry to save the life of a patient. To win this race against death the rider and his horse must be as one and yet the horse must obey the guiding hand of his rider. The rider of course represents the spiritual element and the horse represents the intentional element of man's nature. A better illustration would be provided by certain points made by Ortega in his "How to Make and Break a Nation."[16] This is a better illustration from our contemporary point of view because no doctor whom we know today rides a horse to a sick bed. We shall present the thought of this essay in modified form because we shall introduce the terms *intentional component* and *spiritual component*. However, this introduction should not do injustice to the thought of the essay. For the most part the essay is concerned with accounting for the accomplishments of King Ferdinand and with explaining the subsequent weakening of his nation. Ferdinand overcame the particularism of Spain—the striving of his subjects to further each his own narrow ends, the striving of his intentional component. The king stirred the dormant spiritual component in each of his subjects by presenting to them "great and inspiring enterprises" and by promoting "high moral, religious, and judicial ideals." Thus, under his leadership, Spain became great. Subsequently sectionalism became a ruling factor—or we might say the people of Spain lost sight of these high goals and the intentional component became again the ruler of the destiny of each. Down through the years there has been sectionalism and, furthermore, Ortega wrote, each department has sought its own, narrow ends as if government existed for a given department. We might present this situation in terms of *individual* and *person*, in the sense in which they have been explained earlier. Then we would say that men in each department have been acting as individuals rather than as persons; their intentional components have been the guiding factors and their spiritual components have been in abeyance. Thus they have been seeking their private advantages rather than the welfare of all, as persons would do. It should be added here that it is never possible for a student of Kantian philosophy to suggest an illustration without recalling that Kant once called examples

In beginning his answer to this question of the common denominator, Romero states that "objective culture consists in objective and objectified spirit."[12] He says that this view can be put into "graphic terms, although not wholly proper ones: the transformation of spirit into thing."[13] For consider such cultural objects as a word, a phrase, a painting, a melody, an article in a code of laws, a custom. Each of these cultural objects is materialized but the genuine being of each we do not grasp by means of the senses. As Romero puts it, each has a soul and a body and the relation between the two is different in diverse objects. Sometimes that relation is simply a fortuitous relation. Such is the relation of most words to the objects of which they are signs. Of course in the case of onomatopoeic words there is interpenetration of meaning and sound. Again, in painting and melody, there is a fusion of the material aspect and the psycho-spiritual content. However, whatever the relation between the physical and the psycho-spiritual aspects of a cultural object, "what is essential in each object is . . . that it consists of an objectification and a fixation of the psycho-spiritual; the group of intentions, that is, the meaning or internal content, is that which constitutes the object of culture."[14] It is this content, which is psycho-spiritual, which is the essential nucleus of culture, however diverse the outward shapes which it may take in obedience to the various creators of culture.*

That the ontological nucleus of cultural objects is of the psycho-spiritual kind does not seem so apparent in objects where the material aspect predominates; for example, in such objects as a hammer, or a ship, or a bridge, or a street of a city. But the primary importance of the psycho-spiritual can

---

* It need not cause concern that at one time Romero refers to the cultural object as "objectified spirit" and at another time as "the fixation of the psycho-spiritual." Man, the creator of cultural objects is after all a psycho-spiritual being. As we shall note later, a reason for the creation of cultural objects, according to Romero, is that man is concerned to express what ought to be in an environment which falls short of such achievement. It is primarily his spiritual aspect which sees beyond the given, transcending what is and aspiring to bring forth something nearer to "the soul's desire." Hence what he creates must express the insight of spirit and yet, at the same time, it is the creation of a psycho-spiritual being.

be established in these objects also. Thus one can change the materials which go into the construction of the hammer and yet the psycho-spiritual content remains the same. Any hard and weighty material will suffice for the head of the hammer and any resistant material will make a good handle without the object's changing, so long as it is a percussive instrument.[15]

But the ontological nucleus must eventuate in an outward form in order to be an object of culture and not simply an event in the private life of a would-be creator. There may be many "mute, inglorious Miltons" but, in so far as they have been mute, they have not brought into being objects of culture. Thus Romero suggests that a poet can imagine many, many poems but only when the poem is published in some way and understood by others has it become an object of culture.[16] The publication may be simply a recital of the poem to others but then it is as fleeting as the extemporaneous music of the musician who wished "that the structure brave, the manifold music I build . . . might tarry like" the palace built for the pleasure of a princess. Like the music, the poem requires some form of objectification. Or suppose that one or many persons arrive at an ethical-juridical idea but the idea remains unuttered in the consciousness of each. This idea needs to be formulated explicitly before it can become more than a subjective fact. Again, a bridge may take shape in a builder's mind but it has to be converted into full reality as a bridge which we can see and use before it becomes a cultural object. Furthermore, the creator may not be one person but many persons, as in the case of a language which is evolved. The creation of a language seems to be more like an unconscious development—Romero thinks—than like the conscious process through which a bridge or a poem comes into being. Moreover, a characteristic of objects of culture is that, once they are produced, they begin to exist in their own right; they are independent of their creator. It will be noted that this point made by Romero does not go so far concerning the relation of the cultural object to its creator as does Socrates' suggestion in the ION that the poet is only a vehicle, so to speak, for divine inspiration.

So much for a sketch of the considerations which are the core of Romero's view of the being of culture. Before proceeding we would do well to mention again the essential point of each consideration in order to have it clearly before us. The first is that the nucleus of culture's *being* is psycho-spiritual and the second consideration is that the cultural object must have a material wrapping which enables this object to be understood or perceived by others and which fixes the object as independent of its creator and beyond the process which originated it. We turn now to points which are presented by Romero as having arisen in connection with his theory of the identical being of human culture.

In the first place, Romero states that a major reason for the creation of culture is that man has the impression that the environment in which he lives is not all that it should be; that there is something which ought to exist but does not yet exist. Hence he creates culture: "a vast and compact world of ideas, norms, customs, institutions, and creations of very diverse kinds by means of which he realizes his characteristic being and makes possible each time that his descendents are more truly men."[17] Romero further states that, if the object created is a poem, that poem may be created by one man but this is "not exclusively so for the maker requires an opportunity to be heard." Indeed, "cultural expressions live within a community" whereas such is not the case in regard to mere expression.[18] While this point is not the same as that made by Hirn in his ORIGINS OF ART, yet a brief pause to consider the essence of Hirn's view may serve to highlight Romero's contrasting view. It will be recalled that Hirn points out that overmastering feeling tends to eventuate in expression of some sort. (Dewey would call some such expressions self-exposures rather than expressions.) So far Hirn's view is quite different from Romero's since, for the latter, it is not a personal grief or a private joy that is responsible for the desire to express but rather an impression of a certain amount of undesirability in a given, existing environment, an insight into what is of genuine significance for man and an objectifying tendency to express that insight. These are responsible for cultural expressions. Concerning

Hirn, we have recalled as yet only what he had to say concerning cultural expression. But he makes the further point that a reason for cultural expression in the field of the fine arts is that only by such expression, only by creating a work of art can man adequately communicate his experience to others. Whereas, while Romero recognizes the need for a cultural expression to be heard or seen, the reason is not to acquaint the community with a man's personal experience as such but to present the community with the result of his insight into what ought to exist there and thus the community will advance one step nearer to becoming a true home of the spirit. Of course we must not preclude from Hirn's view the possibility that the overmastering feeling of his poet, for example, is aroused by the desire to better an environment but the point is not explicit as it is in the case of Romero's poet or other creator of culture.

As for the goal of all forms of culture, that goal is "to establish the sovereignty of spirit," according to Romero.[19] Of course the various forms of culture have their proximate goals but this is the final goal, the common goal of all forms. Thus, for example, some technological advances have helped to establish a certain sovereignty of spirit over nature. As a consequence man gains more and more autonomy. In short, creators of all kinds of cultural objects are on the way to bringing about that kind of environment for man which is "not nearer to the heart's desire but to the soul's."

In the third place, Romero makes clear that man and culture are inseparable terms. Thus culture is not an environment to which we may react or not react as we choose but "our inmost selves . . . are shaped by that culture and nourished by it."[20] Romero refers to culture as "a kind of invisible school." The reason for this is that during our early years we are molded by our cultural environment and this influence continues as long as life lasts. Formal education simply "facilitates the indoctrination of the neophyte into the great world of culture." But culture may have a harmful instead of a beneficient influence on man. Its influence will be harmful if the prevailing culture is regarded as the last word so that, as a result, attempts at progress are stymied. Of course there must be a level of culture from which advance is made and that is the value of any given level which culture has achieved. It is when this achieved level is regarded as the height of attainment that its influence is harmful. On the other hand, culture acts beneficially when it "stimulates and sustains the spiritual principle in us with all the contributions of the human race."[21]

More specifically concerning this beneficial influence, literature and art give man joy. Accumulated knowledge has made possible tools and appliances without which life could not be civilized. Religion satisfies the needs of man's soul. Language helps man to clarify his thoughts. In fact, concerning language Romero points out the important function of concepts as a means of making thought possible. He says: "Our actual thought depends on the huge mass of concepts which inherited language places at our disposal."[22] It apparently never occurred to him to think as James Mill once did that, if our memories were better, we would not need concepts. Romero would regard this view of James Mill as due to the atomism of eighteenth century psychological thought. Romero might well say that—to parody a familiar statement—the right concept in the right place is the whole question of adequate thinking, or at least a very important part of adequate thinking. So much for indications of the beneficient influence on man of some forms of culture.

Such considerations make it obvious why Romero concludes that objective culture helps man to live as man.[23] And they also make obvious Romero's reason for thinking that individual man can accomplish little by himself. The culture about him is his heritage. There have been times when man has lost a great part of that heritage and has weakened morally. Such was the case of certain colonials who migrated to the New World. Still further, it should be remembered that the effects of nature do not reach man directly: "they must filter through his cultural medium."[24] We might illustrate Romero's point by a time in Herbert Spencer's life when his health was poor. He was making a practice of walking after the evening meal and his acquaintances attributed his poor health to the night air which he was breathing. Those contemporaries who feared the effect of the night air were influenced by the prevailing view about night air rather than by the actual effect of night air, apparently. In other words, the effect of night air was not investigated apart from the "cultural medium." In short, then, culture has a great influence on man's way of life and his cultural medium even influences his reactions to events of nature.*

What of philosophy in relation to culture? This may seem an absurd question in view of the fact that philosophy is a part of culture but Romero thinks of philosophy as functioning in a special way within culture, as "a rethinking of culture." He says: "Philosophy is culture as idea or problem. The human spirit, which in great part has created culture, spontaneously and even unconsciously, turns above it to comprehend it and judge it, to discover its source, to make clear its ends and to estimate its meaning."[25] In this statement Romero summarizes his discussions of culture as we have been exploring them.

There are two main comments on Romero's ontology of culture which suggest themselves. The first is as follows. By his view that culture is the objectification of the psychospiritual in man we are reminded of Hegel's theory that mind reveals its nature in its creations, especially in laws, in institutions, in scientific, religious, and philosophical theories. Hence these are objectifications—to use Romero's term—of mind, in the wide sense in which Hegel thinks of mind.

---

* It is well to note here that Feibleman includes in his definition of culture not only man's products but their effects on him. Thus he says: "Culture is the works of man and their effects (including their effects on man)." His reason for this inclusion is that "we accept beliefs from our way of life, from our parents, friends, teachers, from all contacts with persons and also with the folkways and artifacts of the culture of which we are to be a part." (James K. Feibleman, "Toward an Analysis of the Basic Value System" in AMERICAN ANTHROPOLOGIST, Vol. 56, pp. 421 and 429-30.) In other words, these beliefs and artifacts of culture become, as it were, a part of us so that we in turn are in part a concrete expression of that by which we are surrounded.

The second comment that Romero's theory suggests has to do with Dewey's interest in determining the *being* of a limited field of culture, i.e., the being of the fine arts, or, as Dewey puts it, "the common substance of the arts." One of the points which he makes in the chapter discussing this theme is that, in the works of the fine arts, there is a sense or quality of "an including whole." Thus Dewey thinks, for example, that in tragedy it is the sense of such a whole "which reconciles us to the events in tragedy." Again, this sense is responsible for the "exquisite intelligibility and clarity we have in the presence" of a painting. Even in real life there are times when we have the feeling that any experience is only a part of a total setting. He finds this idea expressed in Tennyson's ULYSSES in that all experience is represented as "an arch where-thro' gleams that untravell'd world, whose margin fades forever and forever when I move."[26] Now this point of Dewey that a common substance of the arts is a sense of an including whole seems to diverge widely from the thought of Romero that the being of the cultural object is psycho-spiritual. However, we might indicate certain aspects of Dewey's view that bear some resemblance to that of Romero. Thus Dewey is thinking of the art product as it exists in its own right apart from its creator—which Romero says is the case with all cultural objects. Moreover, since the creator of the work of art is influenced by his environment, according to Romero, he would express something of his surroundings in so far as they have entered into him, so to speak. Could not it be said then that, from Romero's point of view, there might be expressed in the cultural object a sense of an inclusive whole? Nevertheless the concern of Dewey is rather with what Romero calls the body of the work of art rather than with the soul, although this point would need further qualification if we were making an exhaustive examination of this theory of Dewey concerning the common substance of the arts.

Another suggestion made by Dewey concerning the common substance of the arts emphasizes again Dewey's interest in the body of the work of art rather than the soul.

Dewey states that "space and time—or rather space-time—are found in the matter of every art product."[27] Thus, with regard to space, he gives as an example of his thought the fact that the witches in MACBETH gathered on a lonely heath—quite the proper place for witches. Again, in time, brooks murmur and leaves whisper. The sounds of music require time in which to be produced but they suggest space too. Thus organ notes may be voluminous. We mention this suggestion of Dewey because Romero has something to say about time in relation to cultural objects. But he is not thinking of time as an aspect of the common substance of the arts; rather he is concerned with the fact that cultural objects have changed our conceptions of time. The machine, Romero says, is one object which has effected this change. In the long ago, when one made what would now be regarded as a short journey, one had to submit to the passage of much time. Hence Romero thinks that man developed a calm indifference to time. But now time exercises a new dominion over us. The agriculturalist has, of course, the experience of olden times for he must wait for the lapse of time between seed time and harvest. But others must reach, for example, the station or the bank at a fixed time. Moreover the letter writer has a different attitude now than did his ancestor for the letter of the man of today will reach its recipient quickly; weeks will not elapse before the letter arrives at its destination. Still further, while time now dominates us minute by minute, the advance in astronomical, geological, and evolutionary theories have given us "a total time which has been converted into a sea without shores."[28] Thus what impresses Romero about time in this connection is not that it may be a part of the common substance of works of art but rather that certain cultural objects have influenced our conception of time.

We have made these comments in connection with Romero's ontology of culture because they serve to highlight aspects of that theory and also because they give evidence that this field of investigation is a very extended one. We are very much in Romero's debt for the way in which he has illumined this field of inquiry. Now we turn to a more pressing problem than that of the ontology of culture. We shall next search for the light which Romero has shed on the current, general crisis.

REFERENCES

1. CULTURE AND ANARCHY, Macmillan, New York, 1925, p. 25.
2. *Ibid.*, p. 6.
3. "Science and Culture," HARVARD CLASSICS, Vol. 28, P. F. Collier and Son Co., New York, copyright 1910, p. 228.
4. FILOSOFIA CONTEMPORANEA, p. 136.
5. *Ibid.*, p. 136. *Cf.* also EL HOMBRE Y LA CULTURA, Espasa-Calpe, Argentina, S. A., Buenos Aires, 1950, p. 10.
6. EL HOMBRE Y LA CULTURA, p. 11.
7. FILOSOFIA DE AYER Y DE HOY, p. 140.
8. EL HOMBRE Y LA CULTURA, p. 12.
9. *Cf.* FILOSOFIA DE AYER Y DE HOY, p. 143.
10. *Cf. ibid.*, p. 144.
11. *Cf. ibid.*, p. 146.
12. *Ibid.*, 146. *Cf.* also FILOSOFIA CONTEMPORANEA, p. 147.
13. EL HOMBRE Y LA CULTURA, p. 12.
14. FILOSOFIA DE AYER Y DE HOY, p. 147.
15. *Cf. ibid.*, pp. 147-148.
16. *Cf. ibid.*, p. 153.
17. FILOSOFOS Y PROBLEMAS, p. 147. *Cf.* also "Man and Culture" in F. Northrop, IDEOLOGICAL DIFFERENCES AND WORLD ORDER, Yale University Press, New Haven, 1949, p. 394.
18. "Man and Culture," pp. 394-5.
19. FILOSOFIA DE AYER Y DE HOY, p. 155.
20. EL HOMBRE Y LA CULTURA, p. 14.
21. *Ibid.*, p. 15.
22. *Ibid.*, p. 14.

23. *Cf.* TEORIA DEL HOMBRE, p. 141.
24. "Man and Culture," p. 392.
25. FILOSOFOS Y PROBLEMAS, p. 150.
26. *Cf.* ART AS EXPERIENCE, Minton, Balch & Company, New York, 1934, pp. 191, 194, 195.
27. *Ibid.*, p. 193. *Cf.* p. 206.
28. ESTUDIOS DE HISTORIA DE LAS IDEAS, Editorial Losada, S. A. 1953, p. 155.

Chapter VII

ON THE CURRENT, GENERAL CRISIS

In spite of all the practical, the beautiful, the satisfying, and the marvelous creations which man has brought into being and which have been designated culture by Romero, man has not succeeded in bringing about peace in our time. In characterizing the current crisis, Romero has contrasted it with two other crises: that at the end of antiquity and the one at the end of the middle ages. He thinks that most men lived through the first two without much reflection on them, whereas today man knows that he is sick and seeks a remedy. This appraisal is couched by Romero in very graphic terms as follows. The first two crises were endured "as one suffers an infirmity without acquainting himself with the nature of the infirmity."[1] These crises were "hardly more than facts" except to a few "superior minds"; whereas today man "follows step by step the progress of the disease, interprets symptoms, imagines causes and effects, and tries different remedies."[2] Hence the crisis is complicated by this "double entry." Thus "just as in a shipwreck, one now has to reckon with the fear or with the serenity of those who comprehend the magnitude of the danger."[3] This danger was dramatized by the second world war, which was one of the consequences of the crisis.[4] Romero does not, however, regard the crisis as catastrophic—as "the downfall of man and culture"—or even as "the crisis of the occident." Rather he regards it as a stage in the development of the occident.[5]

Before exploring Romero's careful analysis of the current

crisis and his suggestions for overcoming it, we shall note briefly a few points made in certain articles published in a special number of IMAGO MUNDI—a number which had as its purpose the presentation of articles whose authors pondered the crisis as a whole or analyzed different aspects of the crisis. The editors apparently feel that this crisis is symptomatic of the spiritual level of the present and that views of specialists on aspects of the crisis in relation to culture are timely. Since our chief concern is with Romero's exploration of this time of anxiety, we shall refer only briefly to opinions of these other thinkers. But we shall also, before turning to Romero, note certain points in Cassirer's appraisal of this time of great concern.

Jean Wahl finds an important value in the crisis for he says that it impels man to examine his values and thus to determine which have eternal worth and which have only temporal excellence.[6] Here we have the implication that man does not know readily what has merit; does not understand easily the fundamental meaning of life; lacks self-knowledge; will be awakened to thinking on what is worth while only by a time of danger.

In articles by others in this special number of IMAGO MUNDI, we find reference made to man's failure to understand himself. For example, Eduard Spranger thinks that we live too much on the surface and do not comprehend our inner selves. Even conscience we tend to regard as the product of our experiences and our environment. On the contrary, Spranger states that conscience is the guide within us showing us how we may live so as to be true to our best selves. Furthermore, man needs to realize his responsibility not only to that best self but also to his associates. He must realize how momentous are his decisions, which have significance for eternity. Only by means of insight of this breadth can he help to bring about a better world.[7]

Sebastian Soler believes that the totalitarian state has been made possible because of lack of heroism rather than lack of liberty; that men have placed security before liberty; that they have not realized that liberty involves sacrifice. He thinks that Dostoiewski's description of the conflict between liberty and material things has not been surpassed. This description is to be found in his THE GREAT INQUISITOR OF SEVILLA. Thus Soler points to man's failure to comprehend what is of real worth for a human being.[8]

Juan Mantovani regards a sign of the crisis to be the contemporary spiritual vacuum. He thinks that this is due in part to the fact that in education there has been too much emphasis on a utilitarian type of education and as a result the student is not integrated; he has developed fragmentarily. As a consequence he does not understand the importance of spiritual values; he is perplexed. Mantovani says that the unrelated ends of such education should give place to a fundamental, philosophical principle. On such a firm basis the student could be educated to endure whatever comes—no matter how critical the situation with which he is faced. He should also be educated so that he can know his duties and his responsibilities. He should be guided out of the spiritual vacuum in which so many seem to find themselves and should be helped to understand the essential, human values.[9]

Thus these thinkers find that there is still need to obey the ancient Greek dictum: know thyself; and this is probably the reason why one of the writers in IMAGO MUNDI has called Socrates contemporary since he—perhaps more than any other of his fellow countrymen—emphasized the importance of that old dictum.

Our next concern is with the views of Cassirer on our knowledge of man's nature.* Like the men just mentioned,

---

* We should not pass on to a consideration of an aspect of Cassirer's theory without referring again to the very interesting Primer Congreso Argentino de Psicologia held in 1954. In Chapter III, we mentioned the view of some psychologists that it would be a very long time before we can know man's fundamental nature. Certain papers dealing with the historical problems of psychology showed the slow but steady progress in the quest for knowledge of human nature. Thus one paper pointed out that Descartes' *cogito ergo sum* is a development of an idea found in Aristotle. Another paper showed that suggestions in Leonardo have been developed in current psychology. Another paper raised the question whether disregard of thought's problematic character might lead to a dehumanized view of man. Certain papers stressed the need for techniques which would yield knowledge of the whole man. Thus, while progress was indicated, the need for much more knowledge of human nature was stressed.

Cassirer holds that man has a most inadequate knowledge of himself. Whereas today we have a "wealth of facts" furnished by psychology, ethnology, anthropology, and history, we do not have "a method for the mastery and organization of this material."[10] Cassirer quotes with approval Max Scheler's statement that " 'at no other period of human knowledge . . . has man become more problematic to himself than in our own day.' "[11] Hence there is a crisis in man's knowledge of himself—Cassirer states.

In order to determine what such measures should be, Cassirer first surveys the views concerning man of outstanding and influential thinkers from Socrates to the present. He finds that great philosophers through the seventeenth century tended to regard man as primarily a rational being. In the eighteenth century Diderot foresaw a new development in the science of man and the nineteenth century brought an increased insistence on the need for basing a theory of man on facts collected through empirical observation. But then the question of the interpretation of these facts came to the fore. How were they to be systematized? Every philosopher thought that he had found the "master-faculty" which would make clear the unity of human nature. Yet these explanations differed greatly. For example, "Nietzsche proclaims the will to power, Freud signalizes the sexual instinct, Marx enthrones the economic instinct. . . . Owing to this development our modern theory of man has lost its intellectual center."[12]

For his own part, Cassirer offers his view of man as *animal symbolicum*. This does not mean that the rational aspect of man is not of prime importance but it does mean that man must be regarded not as a being whose *weltanschauung* is such that he has an adequate grasp of things as they really are or even as they appear, but rather as one for whom "physical reality seems to recede in proportion as man's symbolic activity advances."[13] To understand what symbolic activity in the physical realm means for Cassirer we have but to know his answer to the question: what is a scientific fact? Such a fact, he says, is not apparent to "haphazard observation" nor is it one datum in an "accumulation of sense data." "The facts of science always imply a theoretical, which means a symbolic, element."[14] Thus it would have been impossible for Galileo to have arrived at his theory of motion if he had not first conceived of "an entirely isolated body, a body which moves without the influence of any external force"[15]—a body which is non-existent and perhaps not even a possible body. Now this is a symbolic element in Galileo's attempt to arrive at his theory of motion.

Not only in his investigations in the physical world has man achieved progress through symbolic activity but he has made signal advances in language, in art, and in religion by this means. As a consequence he has "so enveloped himself in linguistic forms, in artistic images, in mythical symbols or religious rites that he can not see anything except by the interposition of this artificial medium."[16] Man thus lives in a symbolic world which is in large part what he has made of it. Without symbolism he would be in a position comparable, Cassirer thinks, to the prisoners in the cave pictured in Plato's famous allegory. Furthermore, through man's creations in the various fields of his activities, he has achieved a self-liberation and has demonstrated "his power to build up a world of his own."[17]

As we arrive at the realization of what man's symbolic activity has accomplished in religion, in science, in language, and in art, it must become evident to us that he is not to be regarded as primarily a substantial entity but rather as a functioning being. Hence we must learn to know him through his work. But Cassirer thinks that we should not seek to comprehend man so much in terms of the results of his activities, that is, in terms of the scientific insights which he has achieved, or the language which he has evolved, or the works of art which he has created, or the religious rites which he has instituted. We should see these as evidences of that creative capacity which has made them possible. Consequently the problem before us, in Cassirer's thought, is to determine the inherent structure of each of these activities and then to seek the bond holding them together. He notes that, in some of these branches of activity, progress is already being made toward finding principles which will reveal the underlying order in each of these various forms of activity.

Philosophy must use these findings to discover the unity of action which Cassirer believes underlies all man's activities.

Thus, while some look to the crisis for the stimulating of explorations to determine man's mental and moral nature in order that this knowledge will point the way out of the current crisis, Cassirer seeks, through attempts to arrive at the fundamental categories of each of man's liberating activities, a key to the unity of his action and hence an understanding of what makes him tick—to use a current phrase.

From this brief sketch of Cassirer's approach to the crisis of our time, we turn next to explore the views of Francisco Romero on the subject. Again we find emphasis on man's need to know himself. Like Cassirer, Romero seeks to understand man through noting what he does, yet Romero does not make man's symbolic activity the focal point of this investigation.

But we must consider first Romero's observations on the reasons for man's difficulty in knowing his real self. Among the hindrances to self-knowledge, Romero regards the following as of especial importance: "the disguising of oneself with a mask," self-justification and the difficulty of making the subject—the I—an object to itself. In clarifying what he means by "the disguising of oneself with a mask," Romero points out that he has excluded from this category "premeditated falsification." That is, he is not thinking of cases where one pretends friendship merely to be remunerated or even to despoil his victim. Romero very significantly says that "such acts are exclusively but not typically human."[18] Instances of self-masking which concern us here because they amount to self-deceit are those instances in which the individual unconsciously ascribes to his actions motives which are not the real motives. Thus his actions seem to him to be much more disinterested than they really are. Furthermore, there is a special kind of "concealing with a mask" in those cases in which one is fully conscious of the real nature of his impulse but unconsciously masks the quality of his act by justifying it "by an equivocation which makes the act appear to accord with the idea which he has of himself and with the principles to which he desires to remain faithful."[19]

As for self-justification, the following indicate Romero's meaning. One may belittle values which he can not attain for the sake of seeing in a favorable light what he does attain by seizure. What he does grasp may be power, which should be granted only to one with the capacity to exercise power legitimately. Again, a man may be filled with such great resentment that he acts with violence toward another. Yet the resentful man may deceive himself into thinking that his act was prompted by the idea that justice must be done. In such cases it becomes evident that self-justification and the masking of one's motives or one's acts are interrelated. In fact, Romero regards the capital fact of self-justification as "the masking of the motives of acts."[20]

Still there are other cases of self-justification. Thus, if one's past has been on the whole blameless, one may excuse a present transgression which is not "excessively grave" with the reflection that he is entitled to commit such an act in view of his usually meritorious way of life. Or one may justify a present ignoble act because he plans to live a practically spotless life in the future.[21]

Besides justifying his acts, man may justify himself or even his entire life. Of course, in justifying himself, one is— in a sense—putting the stamp of approval on his acts. However, when Romero speaks of man's justifying himself, the point that Romero has in mind can be clarified by one of his illustrations. He says that, in self-justification, man may regard his acts as if he were a stranger to them. He may even scorn them as functioning on the plane of triviality "to which concessions can be made haughtily" without injuring one's fundamental self, whereas an autobiography is often a justification of one's entire life even when the writer did not begin his account with such a purpose in mind.[22]

While the foregoing considerations make evident the difficulty of knowing oneself they do not alleviate that difficulty. And there is still a further difficulty: that of making the subject an object to itself in order to arrive at self-knowledge. Thus, if the subject tries to attain self-knowledge during the process of knowing, there is a focusing of attention on the self. Such focusing changes the process of knowing from what it would be were the attention directed solely on arriving at knowledge without concern for the nature of the knowing self. But Romero regards knowledge of the self as of "capital importance" to man although Romero realizes the many difficulties in the way of such knowledge and the vastness of the task. However he thinks that dwelling on the difficulties is not beneficial. Rather he offers concrete suggestions for gaining some self-knowledge.

One suggestion is that a man would do well to decide whether he is an introvert or an extrovert. Yet one should be aware that such a decision does not settle precisely the type of human being he is. For example, an extrovert gets into situations that he has not foreseen and his ability to extricate himself may be due more to the circumstances than to his own character; whereas the introvert avoids such situations. Yet his caution may prevent the development of dormant capacities. As a consequence a man may fail to become what he has in him to become.

Another point made by Romero is that true knowledge of the self can be obtained by combining introspection, retrospection, the concepts which others have of us, and a survey of the ways in which the "I" has expressed itself.[23] The difficulties in this way of making the "I" a "me" are recognized by Romero but he is not impressed by the view of those who regard such an undertaking as futile because of those difficulties and hence claim that man must be satisfied with fragmentary knowledge. Romero asserts that man does aspire to genuine self-knowledge and can make progress in that line.

So much for the obstacles in the way of knowing the self: obstacles due to the masking of oneself, to self-justification, and to the difficulty of making the subject an object. On the positive side Romero has written a classic on his view of man as intentional structure and as spirit. He holds that natural man is intentional structure but that mature man is one in whom the spiritual attitude is the customary one. Man as spirit feels oneness with others. Spirit is characterized by liberty, by objectivity, by transcendence. Spirit has respect for all and interest in all rather than indifference to beings and things. Such indifference marks the natural man. The spiritual man feels responsibility which may even prompt to deeds of heroism and sacrifice. The spiritual man is man as he was born to be.* Such an understanding by man of his own nature is essential if he is to make the most of his life.

Not only is failure to know oneself a cause of the continuing crisis but the lack of a widely accepted world view is a principal reason for the existence of the crisis. It is true, Romero states, that each man has his own conception of the world, his own "vision of things, an order of ideas, and lived intuitions, and a system of valuations."[24] To be a man is to have such a vision and such valuations. What is lacking today is a world view entertained by all members of the "Occidental family."** There have been times when a given world view was commonly held by Occidentals. Thus in the Middle Ages there were commonly held convictions. From the time of the Renaissance there were attempts to achieve a system of beliefs to take the place of conceptions of the medieval period. These attempts bore fruit in the eighteenth century when the mechanical conception of the world, the doctrine of natural rights, and belief in progress gained widespread acceptance. However Romanticism undermined the mechanistic outlook only to be superseded by Positivism with its partial restoration of the eighteenth century outlook. That is, Positivism submitted to the "double demand of proceeding from experience and of yielding to rationality."[25] Newer developments in philosophy have edged out Positivism of the nineteenth century type. Yet these developments have not supplied yet a doctrine which has gained general acceptance. In order to achieve such a doctrine, scientific exploration and

---

* Chapter IV presented a fuller discussion of *spiritual* man or *person*.
** Romero recognizes the fact that some students of the crisis attribute it to economic factors rather than to lack of a world view. However, he calls attention to the way in which one's viewpoint determines his judgment concerning what are the necessities of life. Thus, for one believing in immortality, certain material things are unnecessary. Or he who has faith in progress can forego some conveniences because he has the conviction that his descendants will not experience the same lack. Indeed Romero proceeds by means of many details to call attention to the great influence which one's outlook on life has on his evaluation of the things that really matter.

philosophical meditation together with "tendencies of human life itself must fathom new depths." Surely the fact that fundamental convictions have been attained at earlier periods gives us hope for the future. Indeed Romero thinks there are signs that a new world view is developing.

This world view will be influenced, of course, by the basic characteristics of the Occident: intellectualism, activism, and individualism.[26] At the present time Romero believes that these characteristics are in danger of developing in dangerous ways: that individualism may lead to too much detachment from what concerns all; that activism may eventuate in political and industrial violence; and that intellectualism needs to combat more effectively irrationalism. However Romero does see evidences that these characteristics may develop in accord with current world realities. There is one outcome of these characteristics of which account should be taken in this crisis. The Occidental has wished to occidentalize the world and has been busy doing that very thing in the last four hundred years. Yet now other peoples appear to resent this attempt to make them over on the occidental pattern.[27] This situation presents a truly grave problem in Romero's eyes because of the extrovert attitude of the West. However, he believes that the West, when made conscious of the situation, can adjust to it. That is, the Occident can see the world as made up of different peoples with diverse cultures—all of value, though of varying degrees of value. The common, fundamental position to be taken is that there is "essential unity of the human spirit." Romero has faith that the Occident will come to understand, to appreciate, and to adjust to this situation.

Not only does he stress the lack of a widely accepted world view as a cause for the current crisis but discusses two circumstances which have also been responsible for making the crisis so serious. The first of these he regards as a commonplace, i.e., the fact that our planet is unified by present means of communication and by prevailing ways of travel. Hence happenings in remote areas are very quickly known to other parts of the world. Still another circumstance, he points out, is that each individual has come to look upon himself as the "promoter and protagonist of history."[28] This is one of the reasons for the disappearance of colonialism whereby the mother country has been deprived of resources which she formerly regarded as her very own. Furthermore, before those emerging from colonialism have "set their house in order," they have found themselves in the midst of a world agitated by a crisis. This critical situation increases the difficulty of these people as they try to discover how to use the freedom which they have gained.

So far we have been concerned with indicating Romero's agreement with various thinkers on the point that man does not understand his own nature. We have noted reasons given by Romero for this lack and, in doing so, have referred briefly to his monumental study of man. We have seen that, tied in with man's failure to understand himself, is his lack of a world view. Furthermore, the very characteristics of Western man—his intellectualism, his activism, his individualism—have had as one result his attempts to make over the rest of the world in accordance with the Western pattern. Now that other peoples are resisting this revamping, these fundamental characteristics need to be directed into another channel: that of properly evaluating and adjusting to the contributions which those other peoples can make toward bringing into existence "the best of possible worlds." Moreover we have noted circumstances which have made the crisis more grave: the means for unifying the world and the coming of age, so to speak, of colonists, who now demand to be on their own. Thus Romero has not only indicated causes of the current crisis but, by clarifying it, has made reasonable the hope of superseding it, since to understand a situation is the first step toward rectifying it, as Romero himself has said.

But there is still further reason for rational optimism, as a study of the history of ideas makes clear. Just as a doctor needs to know the history of his patient in order to diagnose a malady, so light from the development of the various disciplines will help, Romero thinks, in knowing how to deal with the present crisis. Each discipline has had or is having its own crisis. Thus newer developments in physics have made obvious the inadequacy of the older mechanical conception. In psychology the failure of the associationistic view was brought to light by positivism and the newer psychology has benefitted by the gestalt theory.[29] In philosophy there have been significant developments. Thus irrational elements of Romanticism have been "domesticated, assimilated, and included in theoretical constructions." Reason, which followed too closely mathematical patterns, is not now so confused. And ontology and metaphysics have recently acquired "greater categorical frames," which may become the foundation for a philosophy significant for all and hence a basis for a new and more adequate body of convictions, a comprehensive world view. For example, the evolutionism of Bergson and Alexander has gone beyond Darwinism, Romero states, and has "reestablished and prescribed for man a place of absolute preeminence in the whole of reality." Again, the ethical values are now being given more emphasis. As a result Romero envisions a new humanism.[30]

Whatever is being accomplished in these fields does not impress some thinkers for they hold that no analogy which will be helpful can be drawn between these fields and the general crisis. The reason for their view is that they regard the crisis as mainly in the political and social fields. Romero disagrees with these thinkers on the ground that such a view indicates failure to understand the extent of the crisis. The seriousness of that failure is this: unless that extent is understood, the panaceas offered will not be adequate.[31] Yet it should be noted that significant realizations have dawned in the political-social field—realizations which are needed in order to determine what future arrangements should be made.

Thus there is the realization that democracy should be extended beyond the political field in order to be "adequate to the concrete human needs," Romero says. Yet he cautions that, while the laissez-faire doctrine has become out-moded, it is today evident that total socialism would crush the human being to the extent that "his functions and aptitudes would be falsified and destroyed" for they need free exercise. Still again it is now obvious that human rights should be adjusted to the welfare of the social whole.[32]

Romero ends this discussion of advances in the political-social field on a truly philosophical note. He says that those who have some comprehension of psychology and history will not be discouraged by the slow progress toward the desired goal. Man needs to acquire a new spiritual outlook, a new way of thinking and feeling and this will take time. Today there are those who urge the retention of the traditional liberties while others would renounce what must be kept of those liberties if existence is to be truly human. These others presume that different goals are more desirable. Romero thinks that the mental habits of each of these groups need transformation through "the impact of facts, the assistance of education, and the instigation of the more enlightened." The purpose to be achieved is "a new social understanding, an active ethical attitude which tends to the harmonious welfare of all and the stimulation in all of reanimated, democratic sentiments for equality, respect for the person, and the continual exericse of liberty."[33]

As for recent scepticism on the outcome of the crisis, Romero ascribes it to a too superficial appraisal of current events. An antidote for such scepticism would be a survey of the growth of the ethical consciousness in the last fifty years. Such a survey would show that there has been a deepening appreciation of the rights of all men. It would also show that the current pessimism of many of even "the more sagacious and the better intentioned" is due to inconveniences that they suffer. These persons are very like the lady of the house who feels that the world is going to pot because her domestic servants are unsatisfactory.[34]

In spite of Romero's optimism, based on his faith in man, Romero realizes the gravity of the prevailing crisis and the need for laborious endeavor to end it. He states that the crisis is ominous in so far as "it is also a crisis of will and effort, of intelligence and responsibility."[35] He evidently believes the old Greek dictum: "In ourselves lies victory or defeat."

Not only has Romero studied very carefully the current, general crisis and then indicated causes and remedies but he has played an important part in resolving the recent Argentine crisis.* As we have already noted, he was a member of the commission which organized *ASCUA*—Asociación Cultural Argentina para Defensa y Superación de Mayo. The *May* meant here was May 1810 for on May 25, 1810 the Spanish viceroy was deposed and a junta took over the government. Though it was six years later that independence was achieved, May 25 is a national holiday. At the time *ASCUA* was organized there was an attempt to suppress the tradition of May and to picture it as very innocent and innocuous but of little moment. Those striving for this suppression were well organized and very vocal. But their claim was unfounded for the tradition of May had as its aim "the establishment of a humanistic democracy." To combat the propaganda of those who played down the importance of that tradition, the organizing commission of *ASCUA* brought together men from all walks of life. The commission drew up a set of principles to which all who desired to belong to *ASCUA* must subscribe. Among these principles the following are of prime importance. The second clause of the principles states that the May tradition emphasized freedom of thought, religion, expression, and of the press. It also states that the people should be sovereign, that the rights of minorities should be protected, and that respect should be accorded the law. A further clause states that the revolution from Spain sought emancipation in five directions: political, social, economic, educational, and cultural. The last clause stresses the need for restoring the federal organization of the nation "at a time of reaction"; of not only affirming the tradition of May but of studying the causes "which have brought about the incomplete or ineffectual realization of that tradition." Moreover methods must be evolved for removing those causes and for assuring the effective operation of the principles of May. Finally each one must consider it to be his duty as a patriot to defend and to make effective these principles and to seek solutions for the nation's current problems in order that liberty and progress may be fostered now and in the years to come. Also there must be devised a method for implement-

---

* *Cf.* "Introduction," pp. 2-3 and Chapter I, p. 34.

ing the orientation of new Argentine generations.[36] So much for some of the principles drawn up by *ASCUA*.

We turn now to present cogent points in two of the articles in the third bulletin of *ASCUA*. This bulletin was published in Buenos Aires in April, 1954. The first article in that bulletin is concerned chiefly with the nefarious regime of the dictator Rosas, who, it will be recalled, was dictator from 1829-1832 in the province of Buenos Aires and from 1835-1852 in all the provinces now known as Argentina. The author, Julio Martino, states that the name of Rosas is associated with inhumanity. It is significant that Martino emphasized in this article the shortcomings of a former dictator at a time when Perón was still in power. Martino wrote that Rosas degraded man in order to bestialize him or to mechanize him; that Rosas sought to suppress free beings capable of thinking and feeling. Consequently Rosas did not achieve the art of governing and thus did not bring about the peace, harmony, freedom, and progress which it is the function of the head of the government to accomplish. In fact Martino states his belief that dictatorship is not a government and thus *rosismo* should be combated by democratically minded persons.

The other article in the bulletin to which we are calling attention is by Romero. His theme is this: "Two Achievements of the Culture of the Occident: Science and Democracy." In this article he points out what the lack of science has meant in the East. He states that "science is the affirmation of personality." He compares the fantasies conjured up before the enigmas of nature by those who do not know science to the antidemocratic attitude of those who accept the authority of one man and humiliate other human beings. He says that "science and democracy are calls to be reasonable and to recognize the dignity of man. This is what the West has incarnated and its affirmation is this: the human being who is intelligent and moral is a person." And thus Romero and his associates point the way to "that pattern laid up in heaven"—to use Plato's phrase. These two articles— together with others in the bulletin—are presented in order to enlighten their fellow countrymen concerning the contrast between dictatorship and democracy. Now Romero is busy with others erasing the evils brought about by the tyranny of Perón. Consequently his contribution to solving the problem of overcoming the current crisis is practical as well as theoretical.

REFERENCES

1. EL HOMBRE Y LA CULTURA, p. 77.
2. *Ibid.*, p. 77.
3. *Ibid.*, p. 78.
4. *Cf.* PAPELES PARA UNA FILOSOFIA, Editorial Losada, S. A., Buenos Aires, 1945, p. 114.
5. *Cf. ibid.*, p. 128.
6. *Cf.* IMAGO MUNDI, p. 32.
7. *Cf. ibid.*, pp. 27-28.
8. *Cf. ibid.*, p. 52.
9. *Cf. ibid.*, pp. 118-124.
10. AN ESSAY ON MAN, Yale University Press, New Haven, 1941, p. 22.
11. *Ibid.*, p. 22.
12. *Ibid.*, p. 21.
13. *Ibid.*, p. 25.
14. *Ibid.*, p. 59.
15. *Ibid.*, p. 59.
16. *Ibid.*, p. 25.
17. *Ibid.*, p. 228.
18. TEORIA DEL HOMBRE, p. 263.
19. *Ibid.*, p. 267.
20. *Ibid.*, p. 270.
21. *Cf. ibid.*, p. 271.
22. *Cf. ibid.*, pp. 271-2.
23. *Cf. ibid.*, p. 278.
24. EL HOMBRE Y LA CULTURA, p. 50.
25. *Ibid.*, p. 62.
26. *Cf. ibid.*, p. 65.
27. *Cf.* Victor Massuh, "Culturas de Oriente y Crisis Occi-

dental segun Francisco Romero," CIUDAD, segundo y tercer trimestre, 1956, Buenos Aires, pp. 52-3.
28. "Diagnóstico y pronóstico de la crisis," IMAGO MUNDI, Año III, numero 11-12, Buenos Aires, p. 36.
29. *Cf.* PAPELES PARA UNA FILOSOFIA, pp. 114-115.
30. *Cf.* "Diagnóstico y pronóstico de la crisis," IMAGO MUNDI, pp. 37-38.
31. *Cf.* PAPELES PARA UNA FILOSOFIA, p. 118.
32. *Cf.* "Diagnóstico y pronóstiso de la crisis," IMAGO MUNDI, p. 39.
33. *Cf. ibid.*, p. 40.
34. *Cf. ibid.*, pp. 40-41.
35. *Cf. ibid.*, p. 41.
36. *Cf. Boletin de la Asociación Cultural Argentina para Defensa y Superación de Mayo.* Buenos Aires, Abril de 1954.

EPILOGUE

In this time of crisis, Romero thinks that it has become clear that, in the past, the universities have pursued ends which were too utilitarian; that the universities have sought to educate doctors, lawyers, teachers, *etcetera*, rather than, first of all, to educate men. Now in this period of anxiety and danger, and yet of glory, man needs grounding in the spiritual conquests of the intelligence more than in its utilitarian conquests. He needs thorough knowledge of the "old and illustrious culture of the Occident." The insights thus gained can furnish a "bridge over the abyss," which our troubled time seems to reveal in the path before him. These insights can provide him with conceptions and norms which will aid him in meeting new situations and which will give dignity to his life.*

That Romero himself has a deep understanding and appreciation of this "illustrious culture" should have become evident in the preceding pages as we have observed the way in which he has illumined some of man's problems. A study of Romero's thought makes clear the fact that he has achieved the ability to see and to help us to see our human perplexities and our human triumphs "desde el punto de vista de la eternidad."**

* *Cf.* IDEAS Y FIGURAS, pp. 135-142.
** PAPELES PARA UNA FILOSOFIA, p. 35.